CHARLOT MURALS IN GEORGIA

JEAN CHARLOT AND EUGENE PAYOR AT WORK IN CAMPUS STUDIO

CHARLOT MURALS IN GEORGIA

INTRODUCTION...LAMAR DODD

PHOTOGRAPHS...EUGENE PAYOR

COMMENTARIES...JEAN CHARLOT

UNIVERSITY OF GEORGIA PRESS

CONTENTS

INDEX OF PLATES

Heavy Type Face Denotes Color Plates

LIGHT CAPITALS STAND FOR HALF-TONES

Light lower case means line-cuts

ACKNOWLEDGEMENTS . . . The University Press is proud to record in this volume three of the most important original works of art in Georgia. The artist's own comments authenticate the faithful reproductions that shed light on the making of a mural, as it grows from jotted ideas to architectural validity.

We have been fortunate in having the cooperation of Lamar Dodd, head of the Art Department, who gave generously of his own time and that of members of his department to this project. We had the skill of Professor Eugene Payor, whose photographs were taken especially for this book, often under difficult conditions. Action photographs, taken while the Fine Arts mural was in progress, are due to Lamar Dodd, Barbara Ormaï, and Zohmah Day Charlot. We had R. N. McArthur, of Atlanta, to supervise the manufacture of the book. His understanding love of typographic tradition complemented happily the artist's urge to present without frills the elemental forms which prevail in these murals. We were greatly assisted by the president of the University, Harmon W. Caldwell, and the members of the Board of Trustees of the Press. The project was rendered practical by a group of interested alumni of the University.

The article "Public Speaking in Paint" is reprinted by permission of The American Scholar, Volume X, No. 4, published quarterly by The United Chapters of Phi Beta Kappa. The technical description of the McDonough mural is printed here by courtesy of the Section of Fine Arts, Public Buildings Administration, Washington, D. C. **INEZ CUMMING**

INTRODUCTION . . . In the fall of 1941, through

the generosity of the Carnegie Corporation, Jean Charlot came to the University of Georgia as artist-in-residence. These three years have been profitable to the state in both tangible and intangible values. The contribution that he has made to art in this section has been vital and sound.

A number of years ago when I was a student in New York I first saw the work of Jean Charlot. It was different—it was personal—it was vital. Recognizing these qualities, I did not hesitate to select this man as my teacher. My admiration and respect for the work of Jean Charlot grew, and in addition I recognized the sincerity of the man himself. If I were to pick from his many qualities one to be dominant, it would undoubtedly be his intelligence. It appears in all he does or says. His approach to art, his art itself, whether or not you approve of his personal method, is never trivial, but has a soundness of which too few artists have been able to boast. I knew that Charlot's presence on this campus would inspire our students as it had inspired me, and I realized the contribution that he would make to our school, our state, and this region.

Charlot was born in France in 1898, and grew up there, becoming an officer in the French Army in the First World War. His family, however, had had connections in Mexico for one hundred years, and his interest in that country was great. After the war he left France for Mexico. In 1922 and 1923 conditions were right to develop the type of expression which Charlot himself says is always present in Mexican life.

The Minister of Public Education became a patron of the arts and turned the walls of Preparatoria School and the Ministry over to the painters. The ensuing activity was largely responsible for the resurgence of mural painting, not only in Mexico, but in other countries infected by the enthusiasm, and for the prominence of the painters themselves — Rivera, Orozco, Siqueiros, Charlot, and others.

Later the Carnegie Institution of Washington included Charlot on an archaeological expedition into Yucatan to study Mayan ruins which confirmed him in his taste for this type of art and irrevocably made his standards in painting those of genuine Mexican culture.

In connection with this expedition, Charlot, in 1931, became the co-author of a book on archaeology, 'The Temple of the Warriors.' In 1939, now an American citizen, and after a career as teacher and lecturer in many places, including the Disney Studios in Hollywood, he published his most ambitious written work to date, 'Art from the Mayans to Disney.' But as the chief occupation of a painter is to paint, and not to write, we find him more often represented in books as their illustrator. 'Christopher Columbus,' by Paul Claudel, and 'Carmen' and 'Henry VI' for the Limited Editions Club are just three of many outstanding ones including a number of children's books in which his work is particularly appealing.

Those who have heard Jean Charlot's lectures will testify that they are informative and scholarly. Yet his greatest and most lasting pronouncements are his murals. Although Jean Charlot has produced pictures in all of the standard mediums, he is outstandingly a muralist. His first wall in Georgia was done in conjunction with the Section of Fine Arts of the Public Buildings Administration for the Post Office at McDonough, Georgia. Next the University of Georgia furnished a wall and sponsored the undertaking, and after days of scaffolding, mud, and plaster, the front of the Fine Arts Building at the University presented the first fresco. A mural, particularly a fresco, as any reader of this book can see, is an heroic undertaking not to be embarked upon with the nonchalance of an easel painter about to cover two square feet of canvas. In consequence murals do not appear at the rate of one a week or one a month. At the invitation of Mr. John Drewry, Dean of the School of Journalism, and as a result of his interest and support, the second Charlot fresco at the University was painted. This was sponsored jointly by the Atlanta Journal and the University of Georgia.

We who have watched the preparations, sat on the scaffold, bothered the artist, and had our knowledge and appreciation grow with the picture have had a rare experience. In a vague way we have wished that all others could have shared it with us. Through the foresight and interest of Mrs. Forrest Cumming, Director of the University of Georgia Press, the publication of this book has become a reality; and through trying times and with untiring zeal she has preserved that experience for all in the pages of this book.   LAMAR DODD

1 · Sifting Sand

2 · Plastering

3 · Frescoing

PUBLIC SPEAKING IN PAINT

In a world clogged with easel paintings a nostalgic memory still lingers of past art periods when painting was a communal need and murals were the norm. On the strength of this feeling mural revivals have been spasmodically staged. Around 1850 the Prince Consort imported to London some Italian muralists to decorate his palace; young English painters were impressed, art magazines prophesied that true fresco would soon be staging a comeback. Later on France tasted in the murals of Puvis de Chavannes as much of the qualities of fresco as can be translated into the oil medium. We experience today another "renaissance" of sturdy make, blown over the border from Mexico.

A mural painting is far from being an enlarged easel painting. Critics agree that there is a mural style, that it involves a composition, a drawing, a modeling and a color that may be called specifically mural. I should like in this article to review those characteristics and to show how they are based, not so much on personal idiosyncrasies as in the case of contemporary easel painting, as on objective physical laws concerning chiefly architecture and optics. If I use throughout as interchangeable the terms "mural painting" and "fresco" it is not that I am unaware of their different meanings; but, desirous of comparing mural and easel modes, I naturally choose to speak of murals par excellence—that is, murals in true fresco. For the same reason I take it for granted that I treat of murals of great size, because small ones do not branch sufficiently away from easel status.

When Leonardo, in a diatribe perhaps directed against Michelangelo, exalted the painter's craft for being daintier than that of the sculptor, he overlooked fresco painting. But Michelangelo, lying on his back on the mammoth scaffold of the Sistine, with lime, sand and paint dripping from his beard, must have been quite as dirty then as in his most dust-raising moments with mallet and chisel. His own distinction, that in painting fresco alone is a man's job, may be taken as his retort to Leonardo. Truly the man that sits on a scaffold many feet high, and matches the strength of his brush against a mortar of lime and sand chemically tied to the very structure of a building, thinks differently from a man seated at an easel timing the swing of his brush to the elastic bounce of a canvas.

The easel painter may, following his impressionist leanings in search of a motif, plant his easel in a landscape alive with birds and cows; if he fancies classicism his work may send roots into the non-geometric curves and non-arithmetical proportions abstracted from the human body; or, if a romantic, his work may emerge from the dark recesses of his brooding. But the postulate from which the mural painter starts is not of his own choice; he is bidden to work inside the mineral landscape sung by Baudelaire, where organic forms and the "beau désordre" of nature or of passion have given way to a rational order, grooved to architecture. Architecture, as its habitat, conditions mural painting.

A building is planned not only as an organism valid in itself, similar to the animal body which does not imply a witness, but also to the scale of its human parasites. The relationship between architectural elements is governed both by "abstract" esthetics and pragmatic requirements. Buildings are made not only of stone and brick, mortar and steel, but of air; their walls, like the wall of the ribs, define recesses reserved for vital functions; their porosity is both the internal porosity of a lung full of air, and an outer porosity, a breathing relationship which windows and doors achieve between the building, the landscape, and the world.

Regardless of superficial "embellishments," the severity with which buildings are planned is comparable in the realm of painting only to the most radical of abstractions, especially those of Piet Mondrian. The people who expostulate heatedly at the rigid verticals and horizontals that Mondrian lovingly rules on his canvases would blow sky-high if a similar rigidity and exclusive use of 90-degree angles failed to be stressed in the plan of a building. The rectangular shapes of the two-dimensional painting in architecture become parallelepipeds, those rigidly cubistic creations within which even conservative people make it a point to be born and to die.

Sensitive to the architectural blueprint that has become his world the born mural painter, following a kind of mimetic logic, bids to complete in illusion what the architect has begun in truth; taking naturally to ruler, square and compass, he will add painted perspectives to the built construction, open or stop the vistas and culs-de-sac that doors, windows and walls initiate. If architecture is frozen music, the structure at least of his fresco will be articulated in musical terms—that is, as mathematical abstraction; the issue of subject matter, make-believe, propriety will be superseded by concern for numerical laws, chords of numbers transformed into clusters of proportions, colors, values.

The depiction of actual architectural elements accounts for a major area in great mural paintings. The background of Leonardo's "Last Supper" is his excuse for painting the picture on the wall. Giotto, Fra Angelico, Signorelli, are all adepts at the wiles of the house painter; with paint they match wood grain and marble veins, the bulge of pilasters, the recession of cornices. It is not only those make-believe architectural elements that cement the union of painting and architecture, but all lines and volumes that partake of geometry acquire in a mural functions proper to architectural members. Ruled on a wall, a vertical line not only obeys optical demands, but upholds as does a column; a horizontal is a level certified by the junction of air bubble and sight-line, rather than the far-flung horizon it suggests in a landscape; the arc of a circle obeys the pull and stress to which arches and buttresses submit, rather than obeying the freehand swing it implies on canvas.

Painters who use geometric forms undiluted work thus in a certain mural climate. Picasso, Léger, would acquire renewed validity if transposed into murals. The painted constructions of Poussin beg to be reinforced by a permanent architectural setting. Mural geometry can be as obvious as it is in Byzantine mosaics or in Gleize; it might also be revealed secretly, as bones are suggested by flesh. Invisible axes pierce the cylindrical bodies that Seurat paints, and inner plumb lines hang from the tip of the conical personages of Piero. In Giotto's "Lamentation" the disciples suffer an architectural metamorphose; they become columns when they stand, buttresses and arches when they stoop. In his "St. Francis and the Birds" the trees are spheres dense and full at the top, sturdy enough to receive the weight of the ceiling. Thus all subject matter, inorganic and organic, conspires in a kind of architectural charade. Even the gesticulations of El Greco follow the secret and severe rhythms he learned in his youthful apprenticeship with Cretan muralists. Even the lushness of Rubens swells or narrows according to a circular or spherical logic, as if the thrust and pull to which the construction submits were featured in place of the construction itself.

Buildings are made of spaces and volumes. Painting likewise deals with volumes and spaces. The spaces that the muralist paints acquire also architectural definition. There is fitness when the space enclosed between the walls of a given room opens into a painted space similarly limited and ordered. Perhaps it is the "open window" illusion, the unlimited space inherent to impressionism, that makes it unfit as a mural language. Ordered space develops by sliding in depth the front plane that constitutes the painted area. This plane may rotate backwards around one of its vertical sides, creating a triangular recess like that existing between a door frame and a door half-swung, as in the "Embrace at the Golden Gate" of Giotto or the "Bishop Cabañas" of Orozco. More often the plane of the picture recedes to a position parallel to its starting position, becoming the back drop of its own shallow stage; a cube of space is created, as if an open box were lying on its side, its opening flush with the picture itself. It is such defined space that gives a monumental feel to Seurat, whose "Grande Jatte" is after all a mural in search of a wall.

A painting can be said to consist of soul and body. In easel painting the body is the canvas stretched on a wood frame and coated with pigment; in fresco it is a mixture of lime, sand and pigment, tightly packed against inner strata of lime and sand backed by the cement, brick or stone constituting the thickness of the wall. At the finger tips of the blind, or bumped against in the dark, the body of a picture is made manifest yet does not function as painting. It releases its meaning only when reflected in the eyes and brain of a spectator. The circumstances that condition this soul, this unsubstantial image through which physical picture and human eye make contact, differ as much in easel painting and fresco as do the physical qualities of canvas and wall.

Easel pictures are conceived as though surrounded by total vacuum. If you cease focusing on the illusive space within the frame and become conscious of the wall or the drape on which the picture hangs, the illusion vanishes. The old-fashioned way of exhibiting pictures on an easel served excellently this need for an unfocused background. Cowed by tradition, the onlooker standing at the proper distance centers his line of vision on the center of the picture, at right angles to its plane. One sees in museums how visitors, obeying a posthumous call, approach close to a Van Eyck or walk further from a Rembrandt, until they stand on the one spot from which the artist guarantees the illusion. The more scientific a perspective, the more the one point of view is important for its effect. Dutch "perspective boxes" from the time of Vermeer display a scientifically correct peephole that ensures depth illusion; lateral view paintings (such as those exhibited by the Museum of Modern Art in its surrealist show) have also a side attachment through which one may "read" a subject matter that remains undecipherable in frontal approach.

Mural painting cannot afford the optical protection of a frame; it has to vie in the allotted space with windows, doors, ventilators and pipes; nor is normal vision and single point of view its lot. It caters to a public busy with practical pursuits rather than esthetic ones and catches its eye more often sideways. It cannot count on the pinning of the hypnotized amateur to the horizontal and vertical cross bars of the median lines that is taken for granted in viewing small paintings. The average distance from which a wall will be apprehended depends on the width and length of the room, the place and number of the entrances, the graded levels of floor, staircases and balconies—a complex planned by the architect and over which the painter holds no sway. Mural paintings have to look well both in centered and lateral vision, from a worm's eye view as well as in a plunging perspective. Such a postulate, distinct from the "peephole" assumption of easel painting, makes it impossible to attain any realistic intensity. A certain amount of artificiality, a style, imposes itself on the mural painter as a corollary to optical postulates. The Egyptian and Chinese mural styles, by ignoring the difficulties of perspective that plagued the Italians, offer a clean-cut solution to the problem of mural optics. But our occidental traditions, intent on defining solids in space, cannot avoid questions of depth. Our mural painter must perforce find a compromise between a standardized perspective based on a single point of view and a mural arrangement that implies multiple points of view.

The armature of so-called "Italian" perspective is such that the horizon line determines the vanishing points and their related fan formations of perspective lines. This key line coincides roughly in easel painting with the horizon line that each spectator generates at his own eye-height; painted and real perspectives merge into one, the illusion of depth is enhanced. Most murals start higher than this eye line. If a realistic relationship is to be kept between the painted and the human perspective, the horizon line will sink even lower than the lower edge of the picture, outside the painted area. Mantegna follows this rule in his "Triumphs" with results scientifically engrossing, but esthetically freakish. In his "Marriage at Cana" Veronese establishes three horizon lines that may well correspond to the true viewpoint from floor, staircase and balcony levels. But as a rule the mural painter, unable to match the painted horizon line with the stature of a spectator, brings both into an arbitrary relationship that results in a weakening of depth illusion—a happening beneficial to the mural because it preserves the physical identity of the wall surface as a guarantee of its architectural function.

The concept of multiple points of view includes centered vision, that is, the conventional way of looking at a picture, and lateral vision. In a movie house the "style" of the screen picture is very realistic and the subject matter is not chosen for any formal plastic value; so that a man sitting on the side sees the picture on the screen deformed into incredibility. In the theater, however, where the actors have actual bulk, both front and side views are equally convincing. The quandary of the muralist is how to approximate the optical results of the theater with physical means resembling those of the screen. To attempt a solution, let us take three sketches of a model, made simultaneously from center and lateral views, and superimpose them into a composite. The more complex and realistic the subject, the more involved and meaningless the composite. Geometric solids with a square or triangular plan would, however, coincide better than realistic subjects, but not perfectly, and would resemble cubistic variations on dice-shapes; and spheres, cylinders, and cones, offering identical perspectives from the three chosen points of view, yield composites as clear as the objects themselves. To insure the readability of his painting from both center and sides (a necessity not of his own choice), the muralist must reform such shapes as nature offers into compromise volumes closer than are his models to the geometric bodies with circular base that solve his problem best.

As the diagonal angle of the view of a wall increases it brings to the drawing itself perspective deformations; side vision shortens horizontals and by contrast emphasizes verticals; to correct this state of affairs the muralist broadens the horizontals. Giotto is so conscious of this that the bodies he paints are padded, Eskimo fashion, with improbable layers of clothes, their bulk further augmented by thick over-all cloaks, their posture stooped until some personages occupy an area as wide as their height. Such stout shapes retain their apparent mass at much wider angles of vision than would realistic forms. This rule applies in practice to frieze-like murals situated in long and narrow halls, such as the arched walks that line inner patios. The opposite condition obtains when narrow and high panels are protected from side vision by recesses, but are to be seen in close-up from a worm's eye view. The slant tends to shorten the verticals, which results in an apparent broadening of the shape. To correct this illusion the painter must elongate his verticals and narrow his horizontals. The elongation of El Greco may be rooted not in a mystical urge but in the optical problems peculiar to the narrow and high chapels of Toledo.

While easel painting is pretty much standardized to a rectangular and a vertical area, the grounds for mural painting show an infinite variety of shapes and slopes. The shape matches any portion of inner architecture, may even drop all reference to level and to plumb line as it follows the spiral of a staircase. The slope spans all degrees from the vertical walls to the horizontal ceilings. True murals are not confined to the two dimensions of a wall, but spread on architectural units in three dimensions. Their shape may be cubical, on four walls and a ceiling, or partly spherical, on arches or cupolas. The spectator, instead of standing outside of the painting looking in, is surrounded by it like a goldfish by its bowl; each turn of the head, each shift of point of view, brings ever-changing modifications to the optical picture, dynamic in the sense that its relative proportions are in a state of liquid mutation. The word coined by Archipenko, "sculpto-painting," fits murals; but instead of covering the convex surface of solid sculpture, murals are laid on the concave surfaces of a solid that is but the mold into which a space-sculpture is cast. In the space from wall to wall, from dome to arches, an exchange of optical relationships takes place. The Prophets of the Sistine, facing each other over the width of the nave, engage in a plastic conversation, start a plastic argument that the facing partner concludes, pair complementary rhythms. In the now dismembered room that Ucello criss-crossed with the martial clash of lances, red on black, such a spatial plastic intercourse filled the air with as complicated a va-et-vient of optical lines as the bounces of a jai alai ball in a closed court. The dismembered fragments exhibited in museums, the photographs and book illustrations that flatten the mural bulk, miss perforce this vital point, and no more reproduce the actual work than a bear-skin portrays the live animal.

Given the size of walls and the distance from which they are to be viewed, much mural subject matter must be on a heroic scale. The aim of the chosen scale is roughly to suggest normal size from average points of view; to attain this aim the painter must take into consideration the height at which the painted area begins, the set of distances from which it will be seen, and the requirements for visibility under the light conditions that the building affords. Thus, though apparent scale can be accepted as constant, actual scale varies greatly, from the few inches in height of figures in Mayan frescos planned to be seen nose to nose by a squatting onlooker, to the giants that can barely "carry" from the heights of the Sistine ceiling.

The actual scale is the one that the painter experiences in the course of painting, and its size reacts on the mural style. Physically speaking, the painter who works on a miniature scale will use mainly his fingers; as the scale increases the means shift to the wrist, then to the elbow and in ceiling work even to the shoulder. The tracing patterns natural to each muscular set differ. Broadly speaking, the painter who paints from the shoulder tends to a large and monotonous sweep, less versatile than the trick motions at his finger tips. When Renoir lost the use of his fingers that could so daintily knot a ribbon with the brush, a heroic spirit came onto him owing in part to the resulting shift in working muscles from fingers to shoulder, a shift that ordinarily takes place when one changes from easel to murals.

The mural problems reviewed so far are not primarily esthetic problems, but concern the physical conditions that govern the making and the seeing of murals. Yet the solution of these physical problems impinges upon esthetics: architectural habitat and multiple points of view call upon the painter to geometrize, impose on his work a style. We come now to problems in drawing, in modeling and color, that are primarily esthetic but likewise so hemmed in by physical actualities, both optical and technical, that their discussion still depends more on objective understanding than subjective considerations. The size of painted walls is such that subject matter, even enlarged to mural scale, will be more elaborate than in easel painting and the dramatis personae more numerous. There are points of view from which the wall can be seen as a whole, optically reduced by distance to what could be called easel size. In spite of the complex subject matter the muralist must preserve in this total view a certain simplicity, for complexity can be absorbed by the human eye to saturation, but past that point becomes confusion. Simplicity is somewhat automatically preserved by the fact that the smaller elements become invisible at the distance from which the wall may be comprehended as a unit. The handling of the brush that plays a vital role in easel painting lacks carrying range in murals. The witty stroke of Manet, the bold brush of Hals, would be dead matter in mural craft. To the muralist the house painter is the better teacher, for he can cover large areas with wise technical impersonality. Having no access to the emotional expression latent in the finger tips of the autographic automatic brush writer, the muralist must find the outlet for his personality mostly in intellectual planning. The vivaciousness that the brush of great easel painters communicates even to bodies in full repose must submit to inorganic architecture. The bloom of a cheek, the warmth of lips, the highlight on an eyeball, lack mural substantiality; at mural range the ovoid of a skull, the cylinder of a neck, express the character of a head long after the features can no longer be seen. With Francesca's women beauty follows mural form and function.

I referred before to a mural composition as a charade where organic bodies and inorganic objects vie in performing architectural roles. This tendency to geometrize becomes much strengthened in practice by the stages that govern the technical handling of true fresco. The painter who dons overalls, climbs a ladder, sits on a plank and paints, elbowed by masons busy with hod and trowel, seems to acquire some of their common-sense manual approach to the craft. To compose, the muralist must read a spirit level, use a plumb line, swing a compass, string a ruled line, slacken a catenary line; to draw, he must stylize a first sketch to mural status, enlarge it on brown paper, retrace it on tracing paper, punch it with pin or roulette, pass it and brush it on the scratch coat, pounce it on the final coat of sand and lime, preparatory to painting. By the time the drawing is transferred to the wall it has exchanged the qualities of spontaneity and impromptu for a dose of impersonal monumentality.

Mural drawing is best paired with a mural palette. Its tradition lives in the books of Cennini and the recipes of contemporary Slav fresco painters. Its sober range owes much to the happy habit that lime has of disintegrating the more blatant pigments, of bringing out the subtleties of earth colors. The resulting nobility suits well the monumental style, unifies in mood and hue the multiple threads of large size composition. Ingres, queried on Dutch genre painting, answered that in spite of its low subject matter its palette was best suited to the noble tone of historical painting. We can add also that this palette is eminently mural. The Dutch painters do squeeze out of earth colors all the nuances that are latent in them. The contrast of a brown against a red ochre in Brouwer's "Smokers" is as decisive as the red-green chord that is Delacroix's culminating cymbal-clash; against the warm ochres a pinch of green earth evokes vistas of trees; on the brown glaze of a jug a grey highlight suffices to pool the sky. Ingres himself has used the Dutch palette when at his noblest but, a stranger to fresco painting, he could not gather the fullness of his own remark, for this palette of earth colors is par excellence a fresco palette.

As is the case with drawing, the technical handling of color has become standardized to maximum efficiency by mural tradition, from the grinding of pigment to a listing of complementaries that contradicts Chevreul's color wheel. The use of verdaccio to underpaint flesh, the summing up of modelings into flat stenciled areas, the exalting of the local color by a contrasting net of colored lines, the open cross-hatchings that result automatically in concave or convex illusions—all these recipes are as human, as wise and as healthily limiting as is, to the hordes of potential sounds, the restricted and filtered range of a piano. If such logical handling acquires today an archaistic overtone that is only because ancient tradition is itself a summary of long-pondered function.

Mural drawing and mural color imply mural modeling, and modeling is ruled by light conditions. The steps through which the drawing passes before reaching the wall result in an emphasis on unbroken outline, the traditional application of pigment in unbroken local color. Such elements could not be featured in a sharp diagonal light à la Caravaggio or à la Rembrandt that replaces the outline with this inner line where dark meets light, that breaks the local color in two portions, contrasted as black to white; nor in the impressionist glare that dissolves outlines behind gauzes of atmospheric haze, splits local color into strips of contrasting hues in its desire to model with color. The mural specification for a clear outline and sustained local color seems to be a frontal, flat, diffused light—a light which best holds the object within the bounds of its own outline, plays low the modeling, increases the hegemony of local color, tends to feature things as we know them rather than things as seen. A cloak painted mural style will be truer to the dye in which its model was soaked than to the law of complementaries as observed in nature by Delacroix and Chevreul. For the mural painter dealing with a remote point of view, such a light guarantees maximum breadth, maximum carrying power. Ingres sums it all up in his aphorism, "Reflected lights in the shadows are beneath the dignity of historical painting."

Both easel painter and muralist work perforce at no more than arm's length; but while the easel painter puts to work both brush and eye, the mural painter can be said to paint blind. If he worked easel fashion on the wall, painting daily contrasts in color, value and direction to please his eye, these many small effects would neutralize each other when seen at the long mural range. Especially in fresco where each day's area is thoroughly finished before the neighboring area is begun, the muralist at work is bereft of the physical check-up that a glance at the whole would furnish, must rely on a mental image of planned results. The daily job will look monotonous until, the jigsaw puzzle completed, the parts gather meaning from the whole. Thus a mural fragment similar in subject and area to a given easel picture will show less contrast both in value and color, less variety in line and direction. This fragmentary state is often misinterpreted by critics familiar with easel painting as a weakness of the artist. People who, confronted by the detail of a Rivera fresco, point to monotony in drawing, dullness in color and flatness in values, do not point to defects, as they think, but to this effacement in each individual score that insures a correct orchestration.

Governed as he is by architecture, the mural painter cannot capture nature as casually or as convincingly as can the easel painter; yet he cannot forego nature as justifiably as the abstractionist. A public building is not a studio where the work of art may be submitted only to the scrutiny of experts; its public is made of laymen who expect its painting to tell a story. Thus the mural artist is immobilized between two contradictory magnetic poles: the mysterious architectonic of the mathematical basis of architecture, and the interesting and clear storytelling that his public has a right to expect. The ancient dignity inherent in the calling of the painter of "historyes" is visited anew on the fresco painter. The hierarchical pre-eminence of historical painting that the 17th century took for granted is accepted again. Walls do not encourage the factual listing of casual objects proper to still life, nor the petty anecdotes of genre painters; their sheer size and their public function fit them better to the doings of heroic characters, to the weaving of themes weighted with human significance.

Propaganda and fresco mix well. In a former day the mother of Villon relished in the murals of her parish church the display of the Blessed in heaven that stirred her to virtue, the vision of lost souls boiled in vast caldrons that kept her away from sin. The "Battles" that Le Brun painted for Louis XIV, the mural canvases that David covered for Napoleon, hallowed as they are, were in their time raw political propaganda. A friend relates an overheard conversation showing that this affinity is still understood, though perhaps stated in muddled form.

"X is to paint a fresco for the government."

"He wouldn't dare!"

"But why not?"

"Because a fresco is a Communist painting."

Public speaking in paint, painting from the pulpit or the soapbox, requires technical achievements distinct from those of "chamber" painting. For even if we admit that mural painting must have a religious or a social content, whatever the axe that the painter grinds it is his job to grind it fine. Thus we come back to plastic problems concerning line, mass, value and color, problems that public and patrons alike impatiently dismiss as studio shop talk. But in final analysis it is on these that the clear enunciation of the theme, and hence its propagandistic power, hinges.

JEAN CHARLOT

McDONOUGH POST OFFICE 1941-42

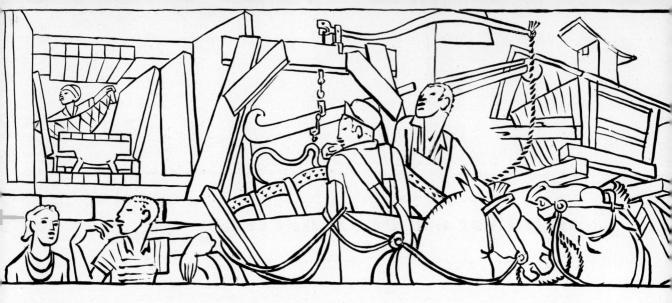

"August 25, 1941. Arrived Washington on way to Athens. Go see Edward B. Rowan to discuss the painting of a mural near Athens." This as consolation for an also-ran entry in a 1940 major mural contest.

Mr. Rowan produced a map of the United States exed with murals, both actual and potential. The test of an inch rule proved McDonough the closest x to Athens. An encyclopedia gave "cotton, agricultural implements and manufacture of overalls" as related subject matter.

I had brushed murals for a government once before, but Mexican officials in the 1920's still disported a revolution-bred informality. In contrast, notwithstanding the genuine affability of its dispensers, Washington intricacy bred unease. The contract entered into that day referred to "The Artist" with quote, unquote and a capital A, a fancy dress for a fact long taken for granted, while the future mural was tagged "WAlpb 3661" which made it all the harder to envision.

"October 9. Leave 7:30 A.M. with Lamar Dodd for McDonough. Stop on way to enter cotton field and chat with pickers. In McDonough measure post office wall. Postmaster wishes a cotton-gin for subject matter." I held live cotton in my hand for the first time this day. Postmaster Wilmer W. Turner, a graduate of the University of Georgia, appreciated the fitness of a decoration. His lead as to suitable subject matter was gladly followed.

The place intended for a mural was a sunken rectangular area, $4\frac{1}{2}' \times 11'$, on the end wall of the post office lobby. Also found there are the door to the postmaster's office, bulletin boards and a public writing desk. But a molding that spans the width of the wall isolates the mural space from its architectural elements. It is further demoted to easel status by a six-inch margin on all four sides, to act as frame.

The paintable area is optically split in two by contrasting points of view. Its left two-thirds is visible the full range of the 42-foot lobby, while the cage of the main entrance obstructs the remaining one-third so that it cannot be viewed from farther away than $9\frac{1}{2}$ feet.

One favorable point proved to be the already well-defined color scheme, woodwork, wall dado and floor pattern all in shades of moss green.

"October 14. Dorothy Douglas drives me to gin. Draw seed house. P.M. Draw scales and press for bales." My model is a building that stands on Oconee Street in Athens. It was my first acquaintance with a seed house, raised on stilts so that wagons may drive under its trap-door to load, with beak-nosed Georgia mules and blue negroes, blue to an eye pitched to the terra cotta of Indian Mexico.

"October 15. Mural cartoon begun." Once studies were secured from nature, the main task was to bind again the painted area with the rest of its wall. To this end most construction lines span the total wall area rather than the panel alone. They yield to the proportions that door and bulletin boards establish from below, concur to shape a pyramid that anchors the mural to floor level. To the same end the lower edge of the painting depicts men seen in bust, mules' heads and the upper boards of a wagon, all fragmentary subject matter that 'spills' psychologically over the unpainted half of the wall, as the spectator reconstructs the missing parts.

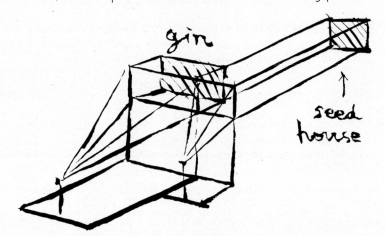

To solve the problem of split points of view, the left two-thirds of the painting is meant as a shallow recess, with the wall of the gin its backdrop, while the right third opens into deep space with a distant view of the seed house and open sky. Thus the contrasting distances suggested behind the picture plane balance contrasting distances in front.

The chosen horizon lies close to eye level, well below the lower edge of the picture. Though such a juxtaposition of both painted and true horizons results in an increased illusion of depth, its main purpose is to knit further both portions of the wall as the diagonal web of perspective lines funnels downwards to low focal points.

Because the conditions under which the work was undertaken implied possible modifications suggested from outside at any one of the steps involved, the less elastic medium of fresco was eliminated. Answers to the following Washington questionnaire make clear the procedure followed.

"Q. What technique does artist propose to use? (Oil, tempera, etc.)

A. Oil.

Q. Method of installation to be followed. What adhesive does artist propose to use?

A. Canvas to be secured to wall with white lead and varnish method, the edges protected by existing ledge.

Q. Give list of colors artist uses on his palette.

A. Permalba white, vine black, green earth, raw and burnt umber, Naples yellow (Blockx), yellow ochre, terra rosa, Indian red, ultramarine blue, cerulean blue, Mars violet, ultramarine red, cadmium red.

Q. State briefly method of working as to technique. (Does the artist underpaint, how and with what?)

A. Full size cartoon traced and transferred to canvas, line marked in India ink. The whole canvas covered with a light glaze of green earth through which the line shows. Values begun in monochrome, light ones with green earth and white; the darks with green earth and vine black.

Next the full palette is used leaving, however, exposed either directly or under transparent washes, the green earth underpainting in enough places to form the key color. Red areas may be begun in opaque white or white and terra rosa, and glazed over when dry with red."

A pencil composition at the scale of two inches to the foot of which segments are reproduced here actual size (Pl. 12 and 21) was eventually blown to a full scale cartoon worked with charcoal, Conté crayon and India ink to insure a maximum range of values. The color scheme was tried on 12" x 16" canvases of details, and the whole rendered in oil at the same scale as the pencil composition.

"January 13, 1942. Leave on bus for Atlanta, arriving 10 A.M. Bus at 1 P.M. for McDonough, arriving 1:50. Show color sketch to Postmaster Turner, to his wife and to the postman. All like it. Comparing it with tinted photograph of his children, remarks, 'Yours is rougher but one feels more behind it.' Postmaster signs document for Washington. Return 8 P.M."

"January 14. Students stretched canvas yesterday. Begin tracing.

"January 16. Tracing, inking. Edna Bartos arrives from New York." A good friend on a visit and a painter in her own right, Edna helped on this preparatory, less rewarding stage of the work.

"January 20. Finished tracing. Lay first coat of green earth.

"January 29. Edna leaves 3:40 P.M. Continued press. Darken mules.

"February 17. Change value of man left background. Lighten value scales. Finished?

"February 22. Mr. Turner here. Daughter Ann makes friends with his little girls. He leaves me their photograph to enlarge into portraits.

"May 11. Roll mural.

"May 12. Leave 10 A.M. for McDonough with Alan Kuzmicki, Frances Ison driving. Arrived 1 P.M. Put up mural with white lead and slow drying varnish. Retouched lower edge. Also delivered portrait of children to Mrs. Turner."

The planning of the picture could receive only intellectual check-up as the work progressed in the studio. With the canvas propped on the floor, the pyramidal composition remained truncated off its base, while heads and soaring perspective at one's feet appeared disturbing elements. Put in its intended position, WAlpb 3661 found its justification.

5 · *First Idea for Mural*

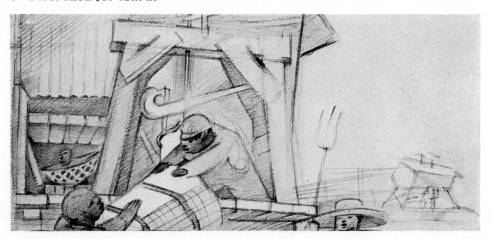

Seed-House

7 · *Drawing from Nature · 9x24"*

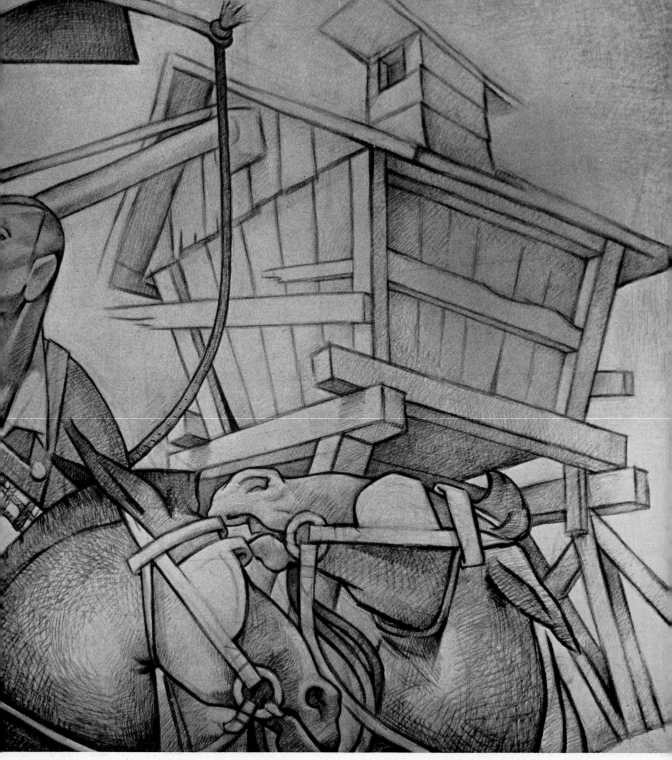

8 · *Cartoon* · *Charcoal, Conté, Ink* · *49x46"*

9 · Wall Final · Oil · 1″=6½″

Mural

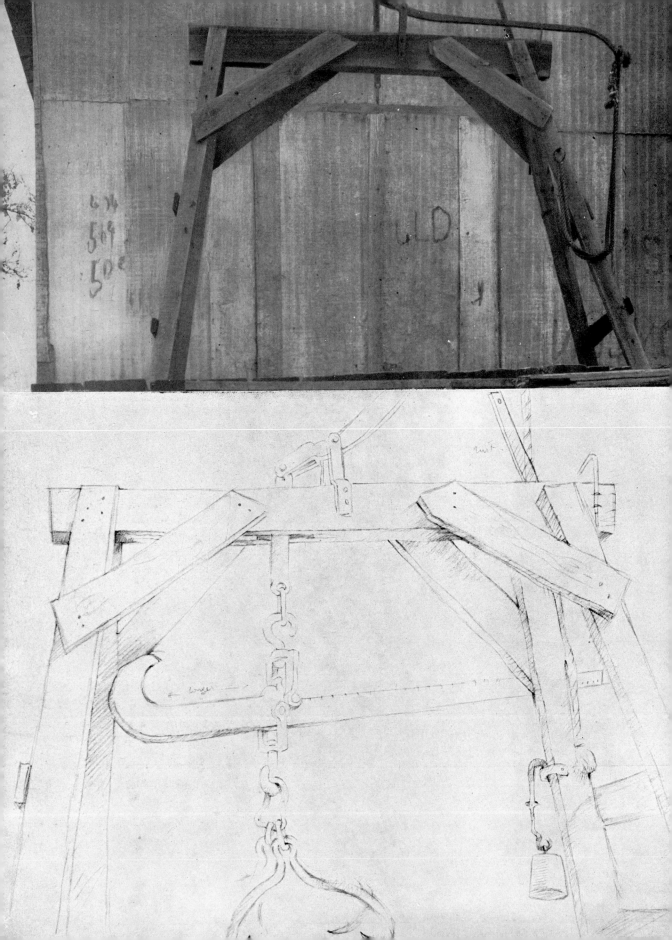

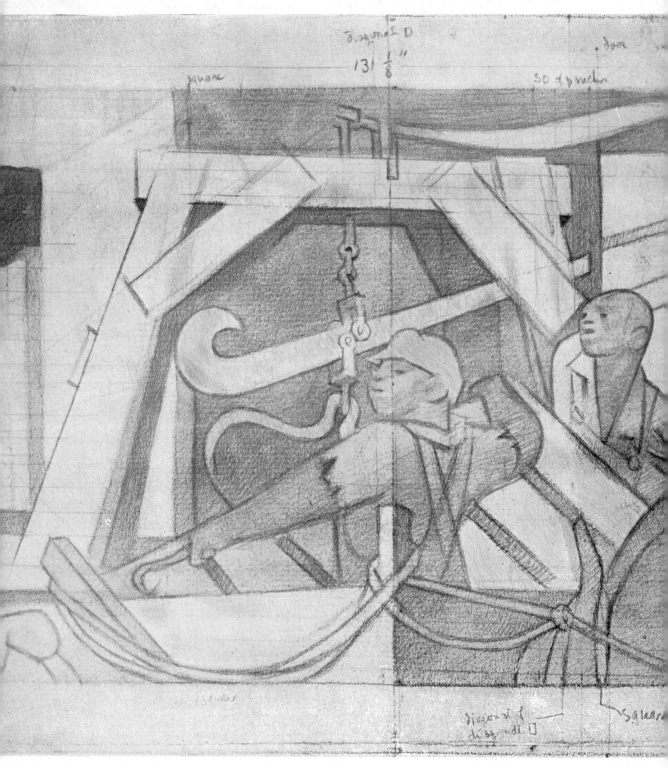

12 · Pencil Composition · Actual Size

Scales

13 · *Central Third of Mural* · *1"=6½"*

14 · *First Gin Hand* · *Drawn from Model* · *16x8½"*

15 · *Cartoon Detail · Charcoal, Conté, Ink*

First Gin Hand

16 · **Detail of Plate 13 · Oil · 1"=appr. 1¾"**

17 · *Drawing from Model (Collection Grace Baker)*

Second Gin Hand

18 · *Detail of Plate 13 · Oil*

19 · Drawing from Nature · 9x12"

Cotton Press

0 · *Pencil Composition for Left Third of Mural · Actual Size*

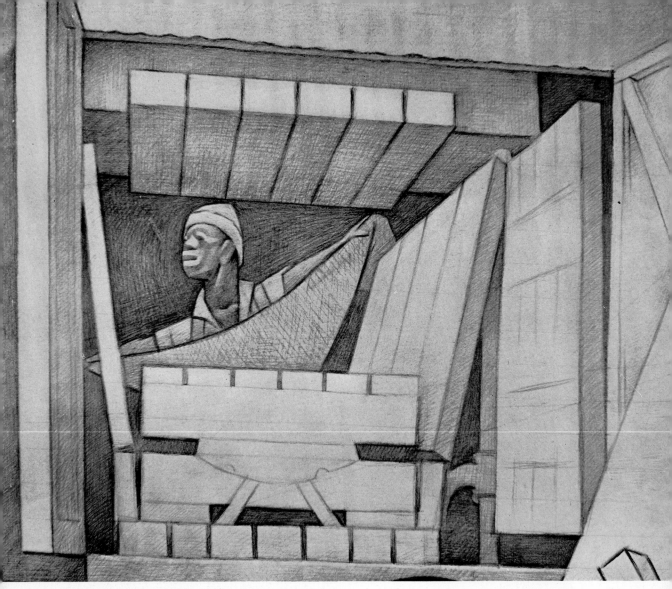

21 · Cartoon Detail · Charcoal, Conté, Ink · 44x36"

23 · *Second Drawing from Model · 17x27"*

Third Gin Hand

25 · *Drawing from Model · 15x12"*

Girl

26 · Color Study · Oil · 15x11"

27 · *Left Third of Mural · Oil · 1"=3½"*

FINE ARTS BUILDING 1941-42

29 · Portico

30 · Scaffold

31 · Wall

Work in Course

PAINTER MUSE SCULPTOR TRAGEDY COMEDY SINGERS MUSE CYMBALIST

POTTER PLAYWRIGHT HARPIST PAN.

On my arrival in Athens, Lamar Dodd suggested the making of a fresco. A tour of the campus guided by Reuben Gambrel, who had himself painted an excellent mural in the Demonstration School, uncovered two likely places. An octagonal lantern shaft in the Language Building presented tempting problems with its optical foreshortening of verticals and eight narrow walls joined at 45 degree angles. My final choice fell on a frieze 9' x 46' that tops the facade of the Fine Arts Building.

The wall is pierced by three doors that suggest a division in three panels. The building is put to a triple use, its left wing dedicated to art courses, its center an auditorium, its right wing given over to the music department. Fronting the facade is a portico supported by Ionic columns that break the wall in three panels from all but excessively close points of view. Those coincidences suggested a tripartite division. The one that obeys the placement of the doors is logical within the wall space but disregards the columns that stand between spectator and spectacle. A correct optical partitioning should take into account the shifting visual relationship between columns and wall.

To this end three key points of view were picked on the central axis drawn to the facade of the building. From each was drafted a diagram of visibility, and superimposing all, a composite was obtained. In it white marks areas seen from all three points of view, light grey the ones visible from two points of view, dark grey those seen from a single point of view. The two narrow areas that remain hidden behind the columns from all three points of view, here shown in black, became logical boundaries between the three panels. On those dead angle areas columns were painted that tie up with frontal and lateral columns. Considering true space and painted space as one, the portico becomes thus an independent unit supported by columns on all four sides.

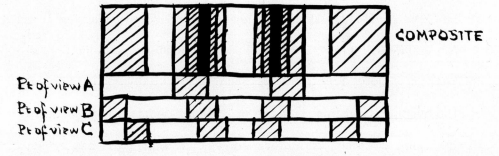

A binding feature was needed to relate optical and architectural proportions. A motif already extant in the grill work that decorates the doors suggested the use of catenary lines expressed as a row of garlands, the lowest point of the curve defining in turn the geometric middle of each panel. They were established experimentally rather than theoretically by easing from each panel's boundaries a slack rope until it touched the door beneath. In the center panel the rope contacted the tip of the pediment, marking the coincidence of optical, geometric and architectural modes. On both lateral panels it fell lower, its curve tangent to the inner slope of each pediment, illustrating the cleft between the three modes.

As to subject matter, columns and pediments suggested a Greek atmosphere that matched in turn the very name of Athens. Granted the uses to which the building is put, ladies in cheese cloth symbolic of the arts became imperative, though held in ill repute by progressive minds.

As in the McDonough mural, though on a vaster scale, the high position of the frieze implied a horizon line lower than the lower edge of the picture. The resulting increase in depth is counteracted by shallow arrangements of drapes that bar the way to deep space.

Because of the size and position of the mural, close points of view are unlikely. Elements of the subject matter were graded after a hierarchy of visibility. From near, relatively small incidents are featured along the lower edge of the mural, the lazy student, the paper chick, signatures, dates. As one backs up and the main personages take the lead the didactic nature of their gestures and expressions becomes dominant. Once past the third viewpoint, as the personages fade out, the two theater masks with their contrasting expressions remain visible. When these in turn become undecipherable the row of garlands carries the rhythm of the mural nearly as far as the building itself can be perceived.

The color scheme answers pre-existing conditions. The ceiling of the portico was found painted a conventional light blue. In affinity with the pool of shadow that the portico normally casts, and in contrast with the violet red of the bricks used for the wings of the building, a deeper blue is dominant in the mural.

Because the outdoor position, even though partially sheltered, dictates a sturdy medium, fresco was indicated. Today water color fresco as Baudouin taught it in Fontainebleau is most commonly used, in which great care is taken to apply the paint without lifting the mortar ground. More rarely seen is opaque fresco, of Romanesque and Slavic antecedents, in which the pigment is mixed with lime or bianco-de-sangiovani. The technique I prefer is intermediate, the wetted pigment being applied with brushes hard enough to raise from the very wet ground a film of lime that in the drying process seals it securely.

Palette: Vine black, burnt umber, burnt Sienna, raw Sienna, yellow ochre, golden ochre, Mars yellow, Naples yellow, Mars orange, terra rosa, Indian red, Mars violet, ultramarine red, ultramarine blue, cerulean blue, green earth. The latter is basic in fresco. Cennini emphasizes its trecento use for underpainting and blends. For this mural three such 'verdaccios' were prepared — cool, neutral, warm — with green earth and terra rosa in varying proportions. A blend of Naples yellow and terra rosa was used as flesh tone.

"December 10, 1941. Begin model wall. Scale one inch equals two feet." This 23" pen and wash strip was the only study of composition to precede the final painting, even though details were studied full scale.

As the work reached the wall, fresco painters John and Barbara Ormaï came from New York to give their friendly and experienced help.

"March 23, 1942. Scaffold insecure. Use steel brush to scrape off outer coat. Wall composition: A) cement wash. B) 2 of sand, 1 of cement, 1/10th of lime. C) cement. D) brick." Once A was scraped off, B was roughened to better anchor our first fresco coat. This proved the hardest task of all.

"March 25. Borrow electric drill. Estimate daily average fresco areas at 17 square feet." Too conservative an estimate as will be seen.

"March 26. Two laborers. One manages electric drill. Draw four heads for wall: Tragedy. Muse Fine Arts. Spectator tragedy. Painter after Lamar.

"March 30. New air hammer shipped from Atlanta, another rented here. Trouble with motor. Draw Sue Walker as comic holding tragic mask.

"March 31. Campus library for Greek inscription 'Athens Beautiful'." The correct text was arrived at with the most obliging help of the Greek scholar, Dr. Bocock.

"April 14. Finished roughening wall. John wets it preparatory to putting on scratch coat, cements gaps until 10:30 P.M.

"April 15. John puts scratch coat through the day with small trowel: 2 of rough sand, 1 of lime, 1/2 of cement. Barbara mixes mortar. Lunch and dinner on the job." Mostly every working day we ate in situ, and mostly every day friends stopped to remark with a mischievous gleam in their eye that indeed we were dining al fresco. The pun palled after a while.

"April 16. Enlarge Fine Arts panel on wall, helped by Lou Tilley. John finishes scratch coat 11 P.M. and dates it 4-42." Aimed at archaeologists digging the ruins of Athens centuries hence, this data was soon covered by the fresco's final coat.

"April 17. Square and draw whole wall, catenaries, etc." The personages were enlarged from the 23-inch sketch, the garlands traced directly.

"April 18. Tried detail drawings on wall with good effect. Draw top catenaries with John and Barbara." These defined the edges of the hanging sheets that serve as backdrop to each scene.

"April 20. Paint in fresco. A.M. cymbalist. P.M. head and hand of Muse. Lunch and dinner there. Tired." Begun in the upper right corner, the painting proceeded rapidly.

"April 23. Finish music panel 10:30 P.M. Tired.

"April 28. Theater panel is finished.

"May 1. Slightly touched top three-inch margin with calcimine. Lighten sky with lime milk. Fresco finished." The painting in fresco of 400 square feet lasted eleven days, an average of 36 square feet per day.

On the occasion of the mural's completion I was invited to talk at a Rotary Club lunch, where I expressed the wish that this outdoor fresco may become part of Athens' civic consciousness together with those other useless things of which it prides itself, the double-barreled cannon, the tree that owns itself. I visualized the day when postcards of the subject, of preference tinted, would be available at Athenian newsstands. Catering to a less extensive clientele, this book is somehow an answer to my wish.

32 · *Work in Course* **(Photograph by Lamar Dodd)**

33 · *Study for Left Panel · Plastic arts · Pen and Wash · Enlarged · 1½"=1"*

34 · Work in Course (Photograph by Zohmah Charlot)

The left panel treats of the Plastic Arts. In it the painter is seen working on a composition, a mathematical diagram rationalizing the proportions of man; the sculptor is seen attacking with hammer and chisel a piece of marble. Thus the painter symbolizes the conception of the work of art in the world of thought, while the sculptor symbolizes its execution in terms of material used. There is also the potter, and near him a potter's wheel of archaic type, a hint of future industrialization and machine-made art. The three artists cluster around a seated woman, "The Sybil," crowned with gold laurels and holding the plumb-line and square suggestive of the discipline and method that must reign even in the arts.

35 · *Lazy Student · Fresco Detail · 1″=4″*

36 · *The Painter, the Potter, the Sybil · Fresco Detail · 1″=11⅓″* ▶

37 · *Charcoal · 19x25"*

The Painter

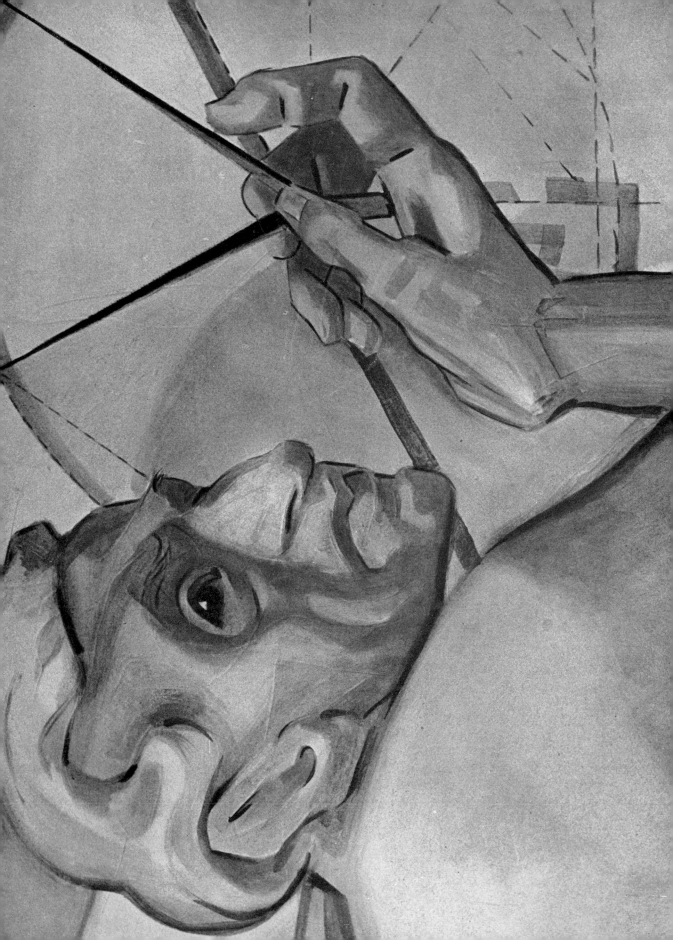

39a · The Painter's Hand with Compass
Charcoal

39b · The Sybil's Hand with Plumb-Line
Charcoal

40 · *The Sybil · Fresco Detail · 1″=9″*

41 · First Charcoal Study · 19x25"

42 · Second Charcoal Study · 19x25"

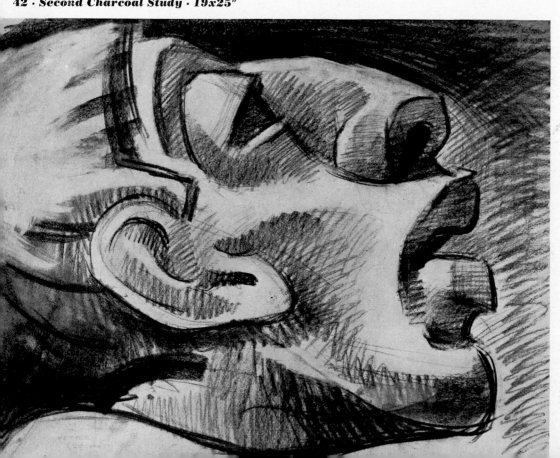

43 · Oil · 11x14" (Collection Earl McCutcheon)

44 · Third Charcoal Study · 19x25"

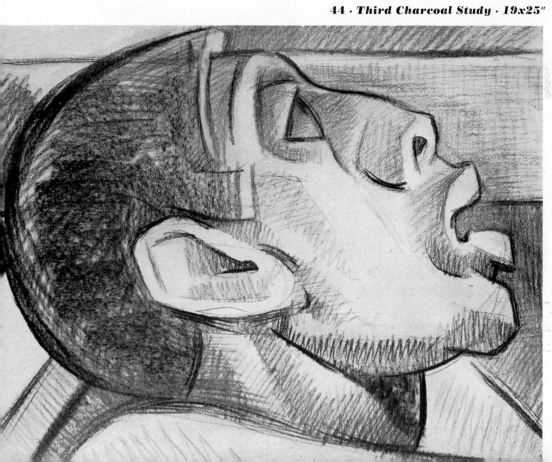

45 · *Charcoal* · *19x25"*

The Sculptor

47 · Study for Center Panel · Theater · Pen and Wash · Enlarged · 1½" = 1"

48 · Work in Course (Photograph by Barbara Ormaï)

The central panel features the Theater. Two women holding masks symbolize Comedy and Tragedy. To emphasize the unreality inherent in stage-acting, each holds a mask opposite her true nature; although persons looking at the mural can appreciate this point as they see both masks and wearers, the spectators painted at each side of the central group remain under the spell of the theatrical illusion, laugh at Comedy and are stirred by Tragedy; exceptions are a child and a dog who prove impervious to this make-believe. Over the middle door is seated the author who receives those varied moods from humanity and returns them enriched; on the scroll on which he writes we read a Greek inscription "Athens the Beautiful," that serves as general title for the whole fresco.

49 · Charcoal · 19x25"

The Dramatist

52 · *Group with Melpomene and Thalia* · *Fresco Detail* · 1"=13½"

51 · *Detail of Plate 50* · *Actual Size*

53 · *Melpomene · Detail of Plate 52 · 1"=7"*

54 · *Thalia* · *Detail of Plate 52* · *1"=7"*

HAND
TRAGEDY

55 · Study for Melpomene · Charcoal · 15x16″

56 · Detail of Plate 53 · 1″=appr. 1¾″

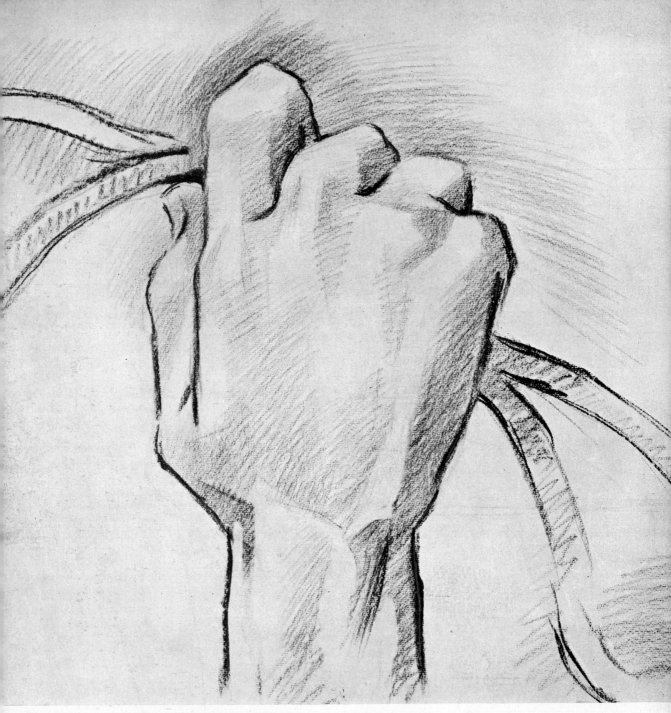

57 · Study for Thalia · Charcoal · 19″ square

58 · *Detail of Plate 54* · 1″=appr. 1¾″

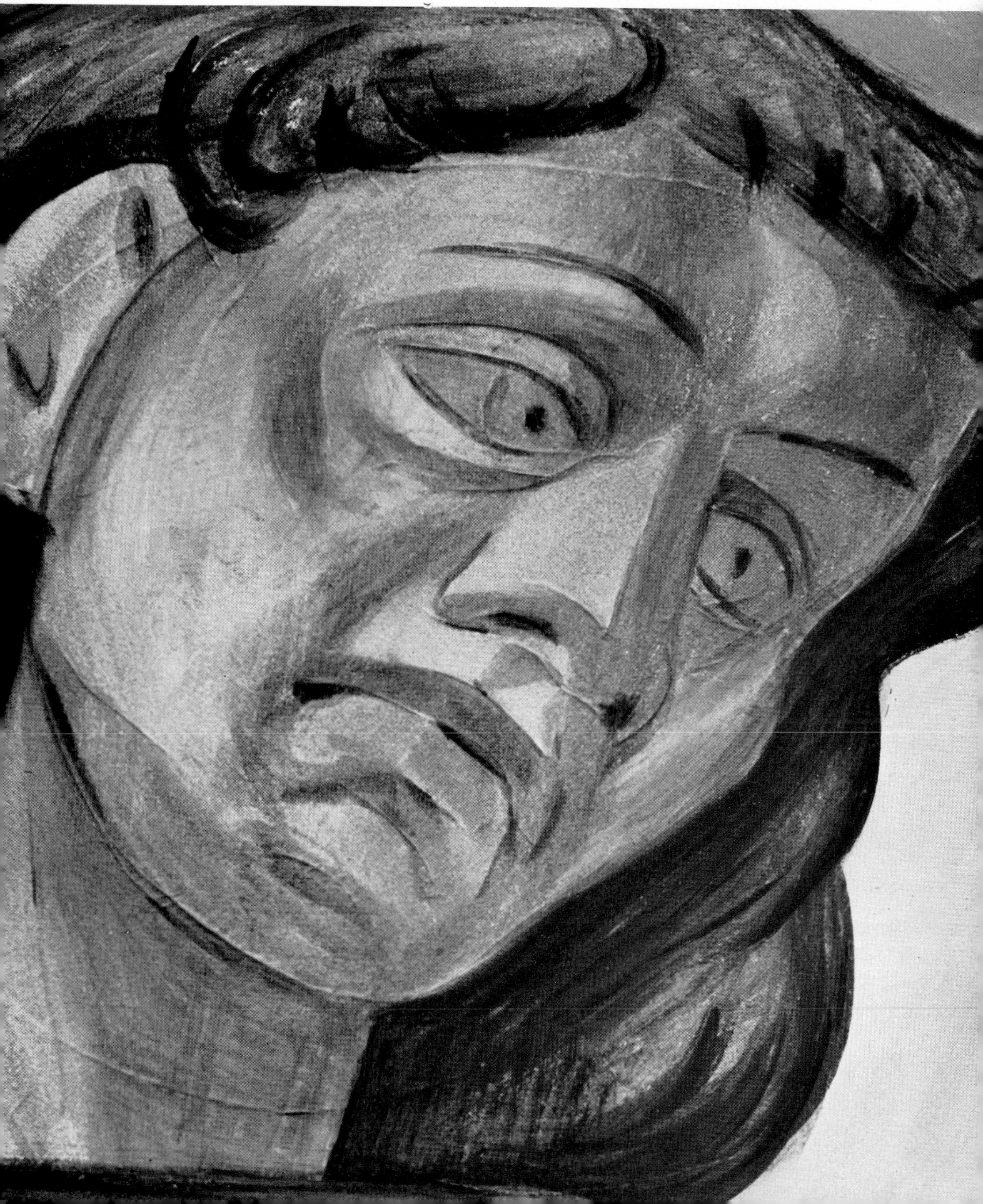

59 · *Spectators of Comedy · Fresco Detail · 1″=9¼″*

60 · *Spectators of Tragedy* · *Fresco Detail* · $1'' = 9\frac{1}{4}''$

Mother and Child · Studies for Plate 59

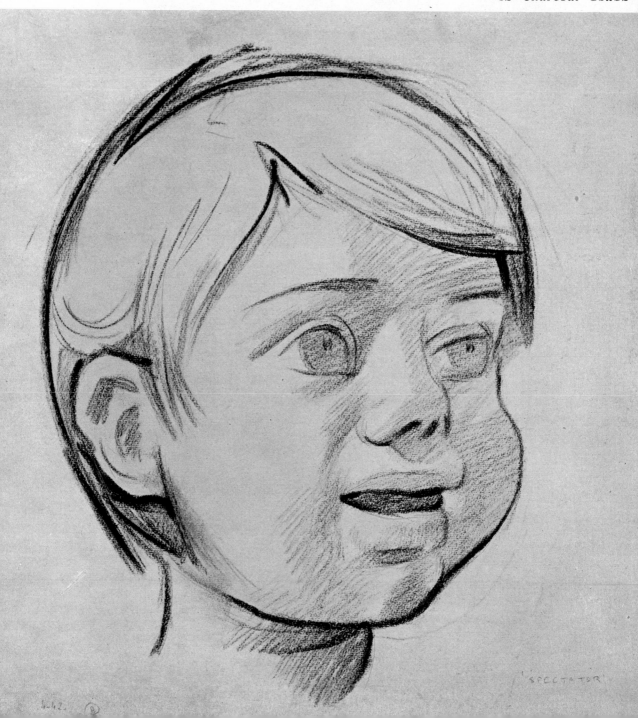

63 · First Charcoal Study · 19x25"

64 · Second Charcoal Study · 19x25"

66 · Study for Plate 60 · Charcoal · 25x19"

67 · Spectator · Detail of Plate 60 · 1"=3" ▶

70 · **Study for Right Panel · Music · Pen and Wash · Enlarged · 1½"=1"**

71 · *Work in Course* (Photograph by Lamar Dodd)

The right panel represents Music. On the right a trio is playing. Goat-footed Pan blows his pipe; half animal, half human, he marks the transition between nature's and man's music; the cymbal player typifies the extrovert activities of music, i. e., jazz in our own age; the harpist, in meditative concentration, represents the introvert appreciation of classical works. On the left a group of singers shows music as a social activity that binds individuals to one mood; the masked singer ties this panel with the central theater theme. All are grouped around the Conductor; with her left hand she beats the meter, while on her other perches a bird that intones the absolute pitch.

72 · Study for Plate 73 · Charcoal · 25x16"

Singers

Terpsichore

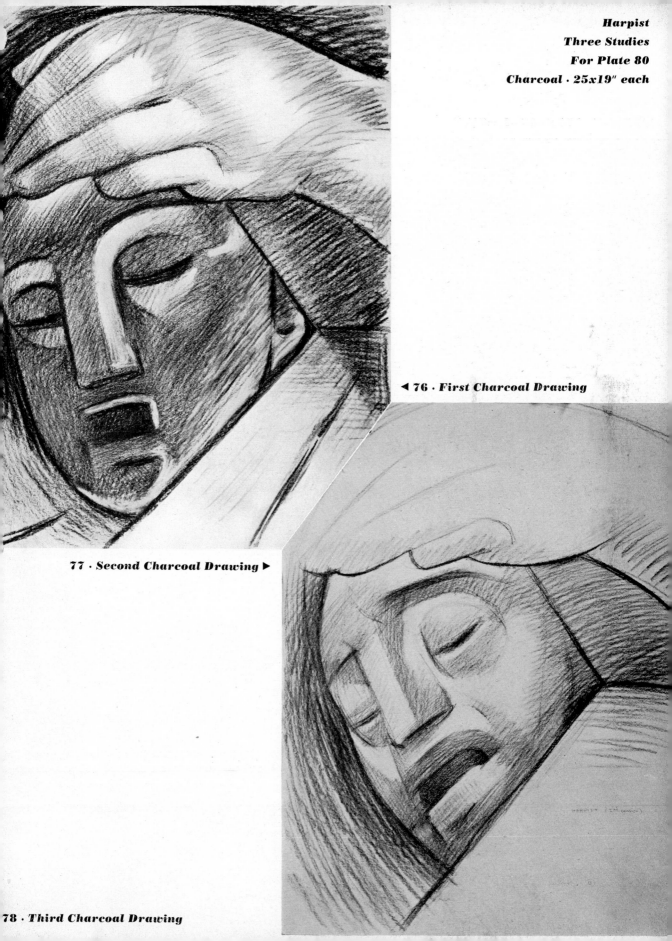

◀ **76 · First Charcoal Drawing**

77 · Second Charcoal Drawing ▶

78 · Third Charcoal Drawing

Harpist

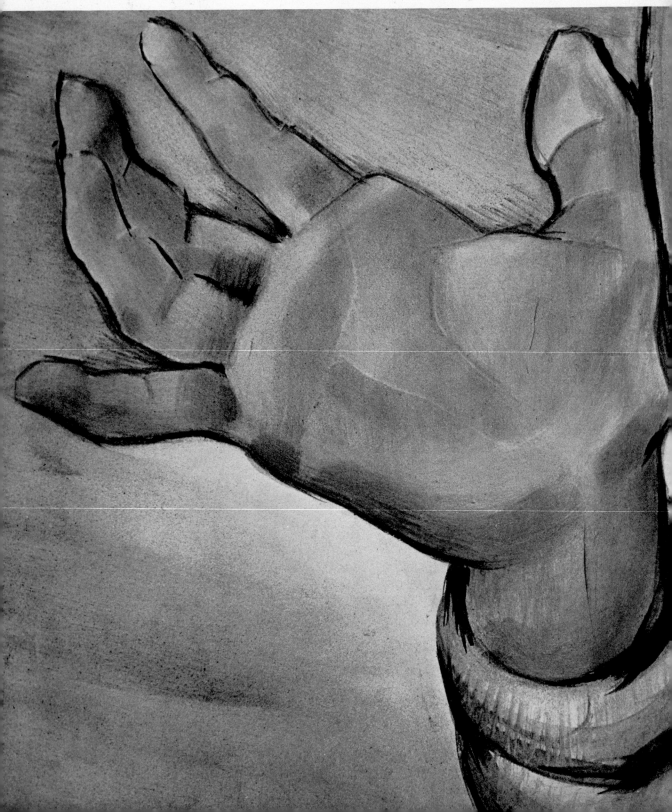

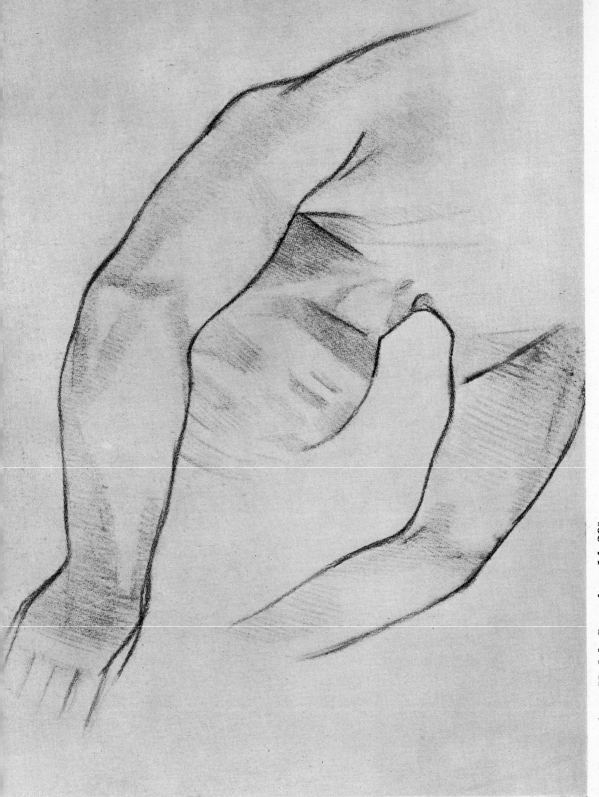

81 · *Drawn from Model · Sanguine · 14x20"*

Cymbalist

83 · Hands · Charcoal · 19" Square

Two Studies for Pan

84 · Head · Charcoal · 25x19"

85 · Pan · Fresco Final · 1″=5″

JOURNALISM BUILDING 1943-44

87 · Hall Showing Wall Cartoon

Dean John E. Drewry had already sponsored three murals on journalistic
themes by Dorothy Douglas Green, Edith Hodgson and J. Chal Vinson
respectively, when he invited me to paint a fresco in his wing of the Com-
merce-Journalism Building.

"August 17, 1943. Measure wall." In it were three doors and an arch,
one of two that span the entrance hall. The area to be painted was 11' x 66',
or about 700 square feet. The layout suggested dividing the mural in two
unequal panels, arched at the top, that fit the dissimilar spaces between
doors. To mark the central door and break the horizontal sequence, a monochrome of a seated figure simulating a statue was envisaged, its head the
only element to touch the ceiling, suggesting the apex of a large pyramid.

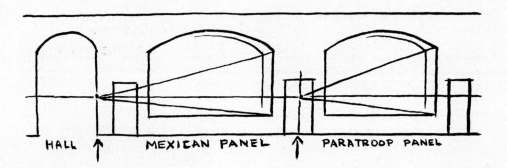

An unusual optical problem was raised by the ten feet wide corridor
that fronted the future fresco, a quota of less than 1 to 6 to the length of
the wall, which makes difficult the use of a normal frontal point of view. In his
effort to lengthen his line of sight, the onlooker resorts to lateral vision, a
fact I acknowledged by constructing the scenes from a sighting point well
aside the lateral boundaries of each panel. An average of traffic habits

inside the building and of likely vantage points of observation suggested as vision centers the corner of corridor wall and entrance hall for the left panel, and the axis of the central door for the right one.

While in both previous murals their high position on the wall brought about a shortening of the verticals from a close point of view, the lateral vision corollary to the architecture of the Journalism Building murals results in a shortening of the horizontals. To correct this optical deviation the figures were proportioned so as to look wide and squatty from a normal point of view, a way of drawing to the taste of the painter anyhow. That such a design may convince in side vision is shown in plate 130, taken purposely with perspective deformations.

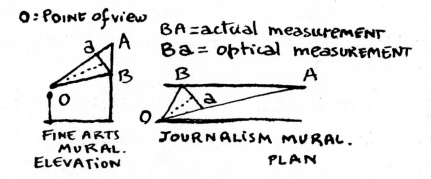

In both previous murals the rendition of depth attendant to their position high on the wall meant a horizon lower than the lower edge of the picture, outside the painted area. The Journalism mural starts 2' 9" from the floor, a normal eye level being well within the field of the picture. This affords three contrasting points of view, plunging on the lower portion as from a raised position, level in the neighborhood of the horizon line, and a worm's eye view on the higher third. These combine with lateral sighting points to give credibility to personages and accessories.

A second perspective, obviously artificial, rules the landscape, that matches levels proposed by the architecture. At left the sea coincides with the top of the left door's transom. At right the horizontal of the river bank is flush with the top of the center and right doors. Established in two dimensions rather than in depth, these lines retain their constructive virtue after the foreshortenings inherent to lateral vision have defeated the realistic perspective established from a single point of view.

The composition takes into account the fact that the narrow hall does not allow a simultaneous grasp of parts, the usual way of looking at paintings. Instead, as the spectator walks along the fresco, successive facets come into play. Contrasts and climaxes unroll in terms of time-movement rather than after architectural canons.

Colors match or contrast from panel to panel to clinch unity for the wall as a whole. Terra rosa builds the ground of the left panel and the sky of the right one, while blue fills the upper left and green the lower right, creating diagonal color directions that supplement the linear pattern.

The difference in panel areas dictated by the position of the doors is counteracted by contrasts in density. The wider left panel holds loosely grouped large forms with weak value contrasts, the smaller right panel is tightly packed with thin forms, uses as recurrent motif white straps in decided value contrast with a darker ground.

"August 18. Consult John Drewry as to subject matter." A desire to try my hand again at a theme I had frescoed more than twenty years ago suggested the conquest of Mexico for the left panel. We chose as its counterpart the conquest of Europe by American paratroopers. An allowance was made for the expected connection with journalism.

"August 21. Plan wall to the scale of 1 inch to the foot. Begin with Indian group and block in conquistadores in water color.

"September 26. Begin geometry on wall with Mary Taylor and Edith Hodgson. Place Indian group." The wall was of a light creamy finish, of a texture that took pencil so well that I planned the cartoon directly on it. This allowed for a mural feel from the start, helped solve in situ problems relating to sideway vision and perspective levels. A handicap was that the elaborate cartoon, "biggest pencil sketch in the world" as a press release worded it, was doomed to destruction before the fresco could start. Facsimile copies of details and an allover tracing preserved the necessary data, together with photographs mapping to scale the whole area, taken by Eugene Payor. He further volunteered to letter all captions.

Though I could produce most of the Mexican story by rote, the steeds of the Spaniards were inspired by a single farm-horse, Pearl by name, that I met on the grounds of Black Mountain College in the fall of 1943.

The war panel was new material. To gather data towards its completion, Dean Drewry arranged for my visit to a paratroop training school where maneuvers were held under combat conditions.

TS COVER AMERIC

"November 3. Leave 8:40 A.M. Columbus 4:30 P.M. City bus to Fort Benning. Captain Spitzer. Lt. Lemon. Room with Lt. Sheean.

"November 4. To Alabama Field to watch parachute mass landings. Meet Lt. Schultz. Beautiful profile as he uses walkie-talkie. Calculation of landing spot in relation to position airplane based on wind and speed. Am on the field as they land. The combat parachute is green. In the air feet apart, feet together at landing. Often land in trees, feet crossed and arms protecting face, parachute drapes on tree.

"Two buckles to unhook, at breast and groin. Emergency parachute hooks in front slightly lower than breast buckle. After landing, crouch and drop flat or roll.

"P.M. With Sgt. Beck until 6 P.M. Good drawings. Return in truck. Evening, tint drawings made this afternoon.

"November 5. Morning to 'bundle' department. Sketch unpacking and mounting of 81 millimeter mortar. 2 P.M. camouflage section. Sketch war paint. 4 P.M. to jump towers. Leave tomorrow.

"November 6. Arrive Athens 5:30 P.M. Long letter from Stanton Forbes on colored marble dust and asbestos fiber to mix with mortar.

"November 8. Begin left second panel: press corner and 'Deposition'.

"November 20. Finish cartoon second panel.

"December 8. Plan daily areas. Left panel 25. Right panel 22. Center 3. Total 50." I guessed right for the central figure but worked only 16 days on each panel, or a total of 35 working days.

"December 27. A.M. Meet master mason. P.M. With two helpers has chopped down most of the paratrooper cartoon." Roy Garren proved a valuable assistant and developed a fondness for fresco that vied with his other avocation, rabbit-hunting.

"December 30. Wall completely scraped. Begin geometric draft on same with Zohmah.

"December 31. Wall somewhat of a problem. It contains sand, plaster and detritus of rope, straw, horsehair. Mason suggests an intermediate coat between this and final layer." A blend of sand, plaster and lime eased the transition between the wall as found and the final coat of lime and sand, an important technical step.

"January 3. Trace and paint area 1 with two colors only, cerulean and black, with lime highlights." On this first day I painted the head of the statue. From there the work spread top right and left to the simulated arches and uprights through which the two scenes are viewed. To differentiate it from the panels proper this make-believe architecture is not brushed in, but is an inlay of dark and light mortar.

"January 6. Lorraine Harris grinds new Weber colors just received: burnt green earth, oxide of chromium, intense green, cadmium red." These colors completed a palette made of the leftover pigments already listed in connection with the Fine Arts Building fresco.

The painting proceeded by horizontal strata spanning the wall, regardless of its division into panels. Though it helped unify the design as a whole, intervals of weeks elapsed before pieces of one body or even one face were joined on the vertical.

Sample entries: "January 19. Panel I, area 3. Woman offering garland, burnt green earth. Woman offering 'batea,' Mars violet. Front porter laid on with cerulean blue, washed over in shadows with Mars violet. Harris lays the sea ultramarine. Zohmah brings sandwiches at noon. Finish 7:15 P.M.

PANEL I. AREA 3.

"February 3. Panel 2, area 10. Schultz at the walkie-talkie. Use tracing, drawing and oil painting for guides. Face underpainted with blend of green earth and burnt green earth. Darks green earth, lines in raw umber. Gloves same blend as face. Walkie-talkie green earth and raw umber. Light on strap yellow ochre, darks in raw umber. Uniform in green earth with a little ultramarine blue."

The hind part of a dog barking at a horse was painted January 21st. "February 22. Panel I, area 16. Paint center horse and front part of dog. Harris paints landscape and ground. For horse, verdaccio and Naples yellow mixed with palette knife, cool verdaccio for darks. Saddle cloth ultramarine red, reins terra rosa, burnt Sienna. Dog ultramarine blue, burnt Sienna. This ends painting proper."

Retouchings of two kinds followed. Drastic ones, by knocking down doubtful areas and painting anew on fresh mortar. Lighter retouching was in secco, painting on the dry ground with pigment mixed with milk of lime.

The work of painting 700 square feet lasted 35 working days, an average of 20 square feet a day.

"February 29. Eugene Payor letters first line of dedication plaque." The completed inscription reads:

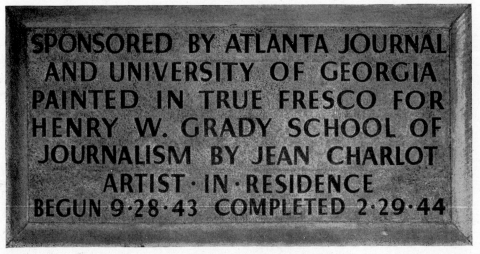

SPONSORED BY ATLANTA JOURNAL AND UNIVERSITY OF GEORGIA PAINTED IN TRUE FRESCO FOR HENRY W. GRADY SCHOOL OF JOURNALISM BY JEAN CHARLOT ARTIST·IN·RESIDENCE BEGUN 9·28·43 COMPLETED 2·29·44

90 ·

Same day, "Surprise party to celebrate completion mural. Lunch in Hall of Fame. Very good salad mixed by Rita Payor. Very good cake with two candles baked by Lorraine Harris inscribed: 'Charlot mural' and 'Baby Charlot'. Garren joins us. All very gracious."

Martin Peter Day Charlot was born 1:02 A.M., March 6, five days after the birth of the fresco.

**91
Destroying
Cartoon**

**92
Fresco
in
Course**

**93
Martin
Charlot**

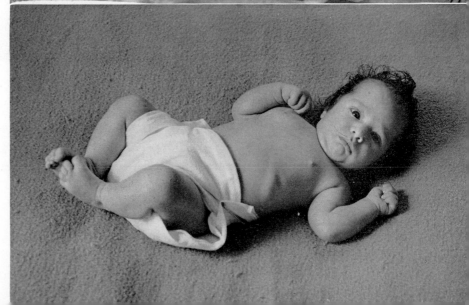

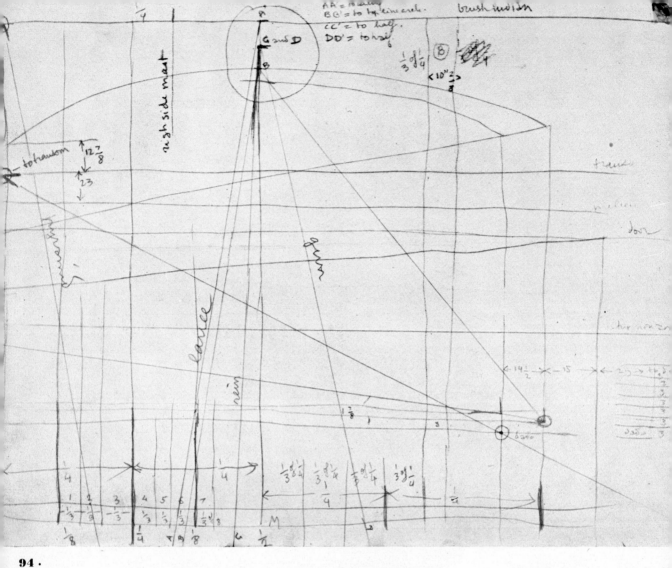

ANNO DMI. 1519. EMPEROR MONTEZUMA'S SCOUTS COVER
AMERICA'S FIRST SCOOP. CORTEZ IN MEXICO. When Cortez landed
in the port that came to be known as Vera Cruz, the Aztec emperor, ad-
vised by runners of the arrival of the strangers, dispatched court artists to
make sketches of the odd Spaniards, their boats, horses, armors. He also
sent an envoy, chosen for magical reasons as his physical double, to greet
the small party. The Aztec drawings in this fresco are free copies of orig-
inals still preserved.

On the Spanish side, Cortez is portrayed after his likeness preserved in Mexico City in a hospital he endowed. One recognizes also Alvarado, nicknamed "Sun God" by the Indians awed by his flaming hair. Even the horses are portraits, as penned by Bernal Diaz del Castillo," Alonso Hernandez de Puerto Carrero's gray mare, a good charger, which Cortez bought for him with his gold buttons. Juan Velasquez de Leon's, another very powerful gray mare we called 'bob-tailed'; very handy and a good charger. Diego de Ordaz' gray mare, barren, fairly good, even though it did not run much."

While the artists paint, their women folk prepare tortillas, the maize cake that is still a mainstay of Mexican diet, and children busy themselves with a bug.

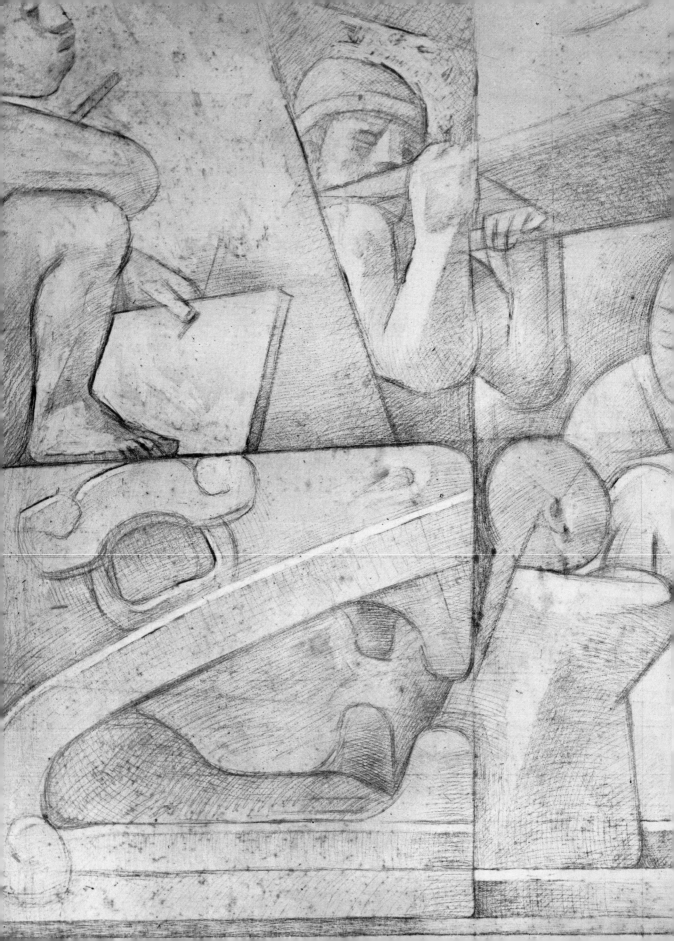

96 · *Indian Scribe* · *Fresco Detail* · $1'' = 3\frac{1}{2}''$

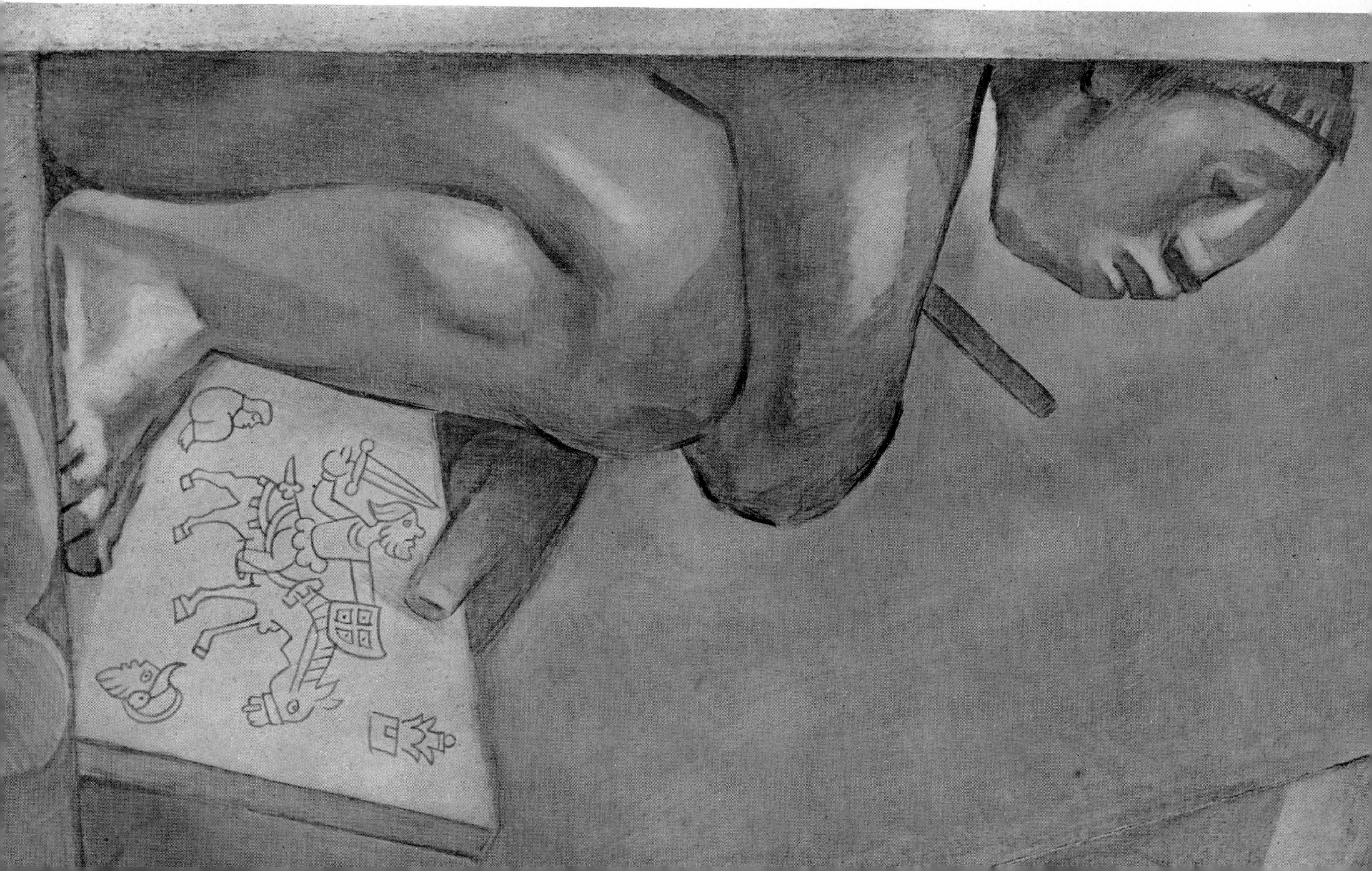

97 · *Scribe's Head · Actual Size*

Two Details from Plate 96

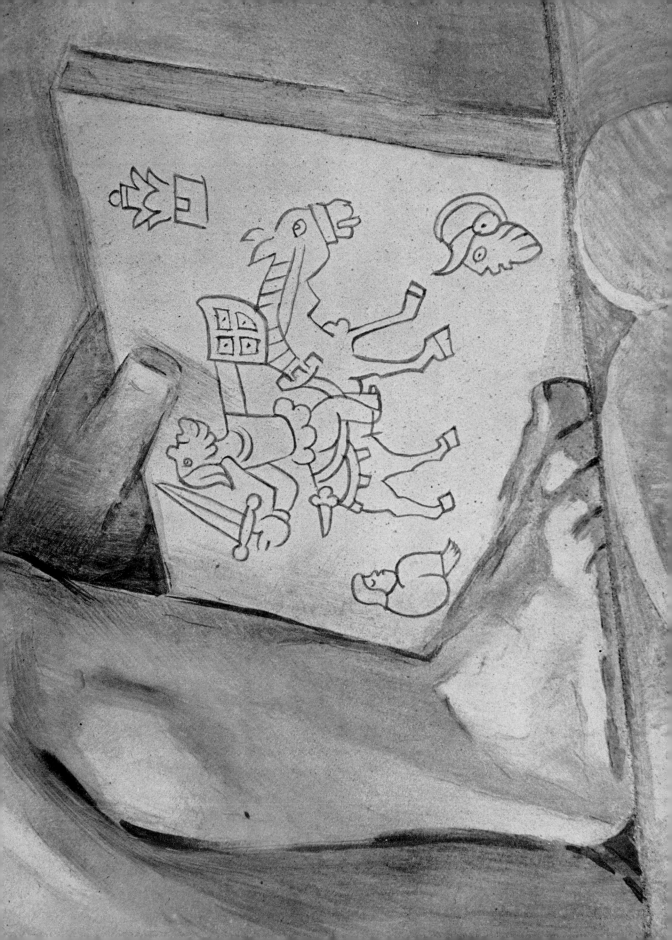

101 · Fresco Final · 1″=6′

102 · Cartoon Detail · Pencil

105 · *Front Porter*

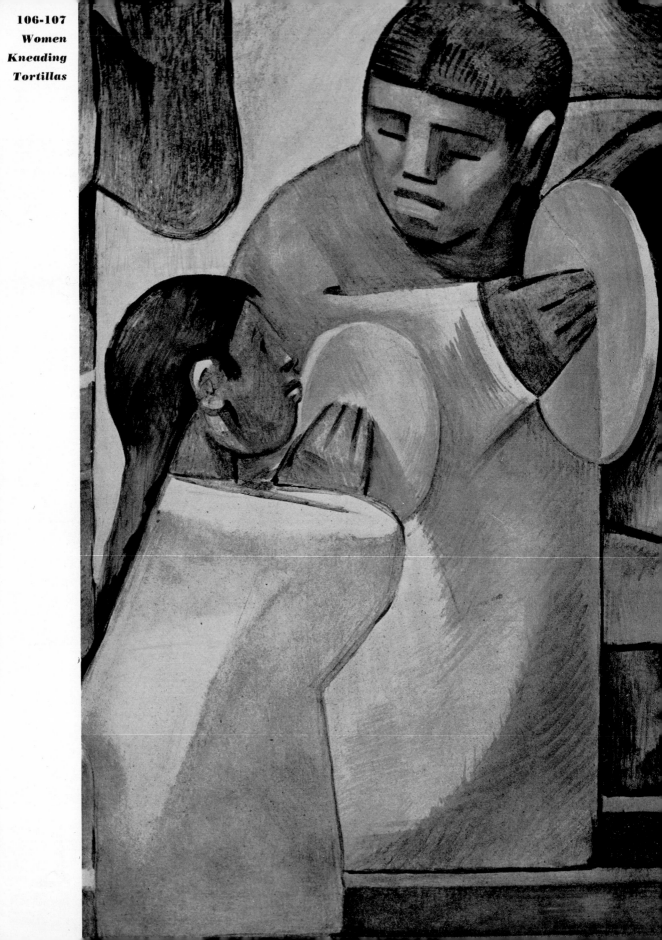

**Fresco
Detail
1"=4"**

Gift Bearers

110 · *Woman with Garland* · 1″＝2″

Two Details from Plate 109

112 · Conquistadores · First Idea · Pencil · 8x12"

Alvarado

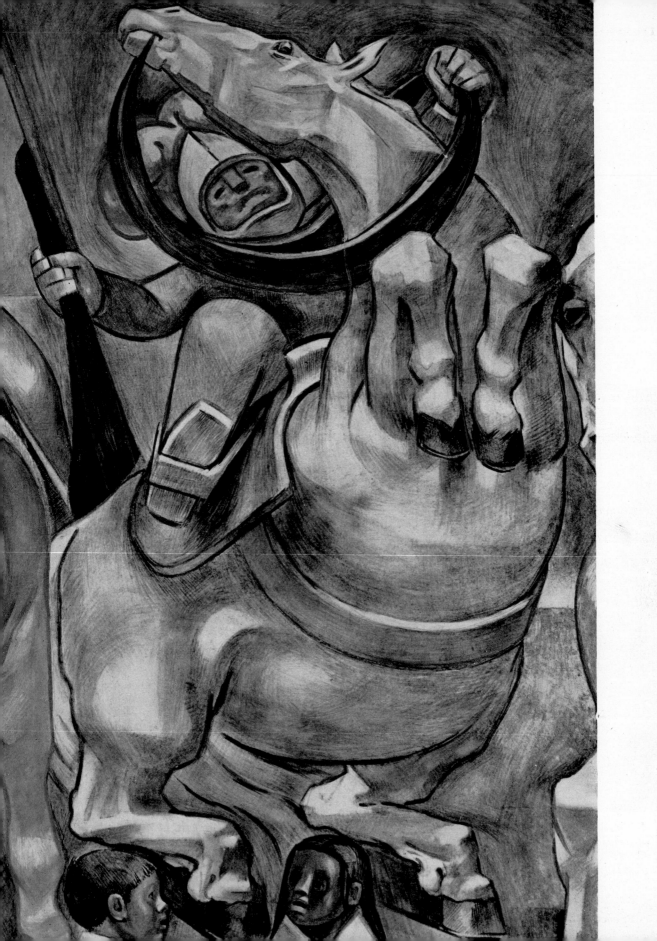

Conquistador

117 · *Study from Model for Plate 116 · Black Mountain · 9x12"*

119 · *Cartoon for Plate 118 · Pencil · 16x25"*

Cortez' Horse

122 · Study from Model for Plate 123 · Black Mountain · 10½x8″

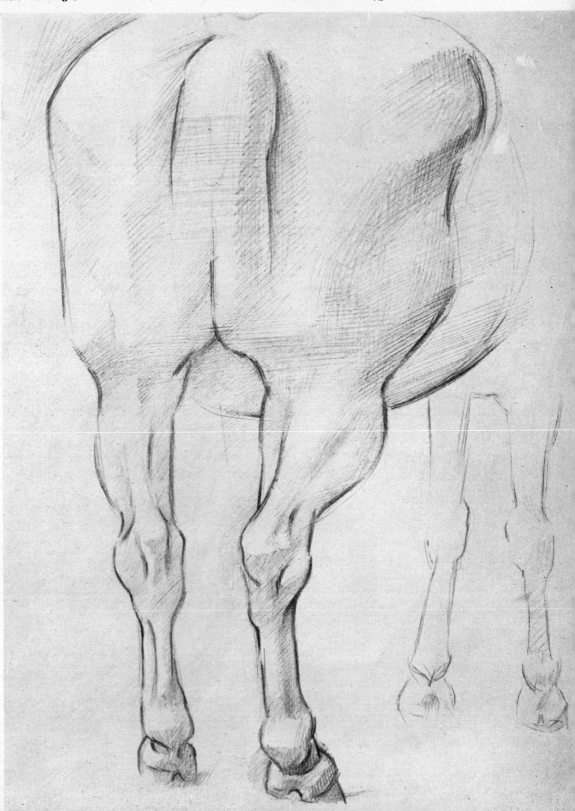

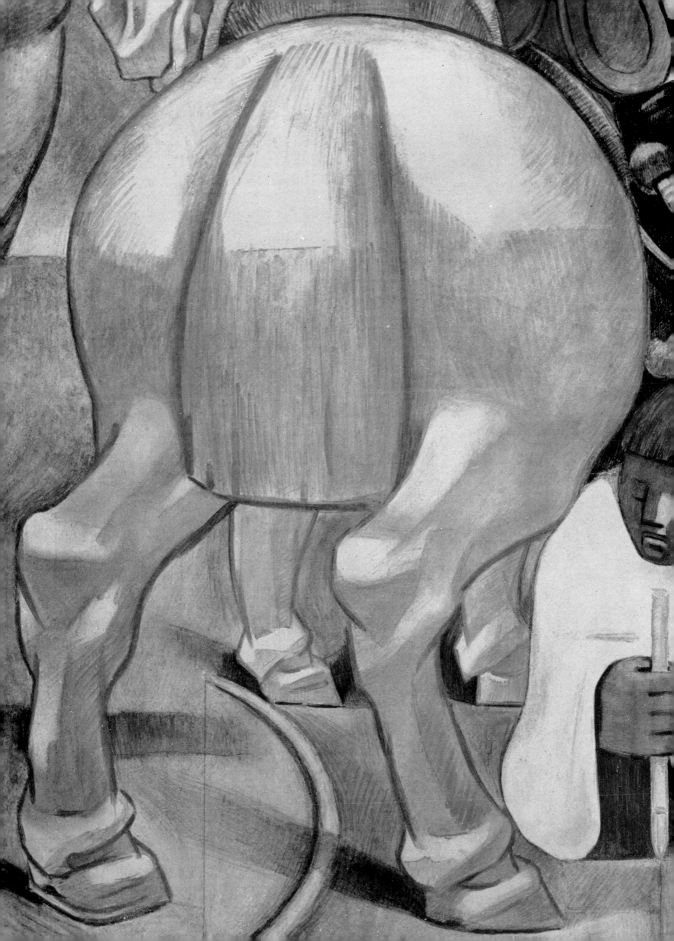

124 · *Cortez' Horse* · *Fresco Detail* · *1"=3"*

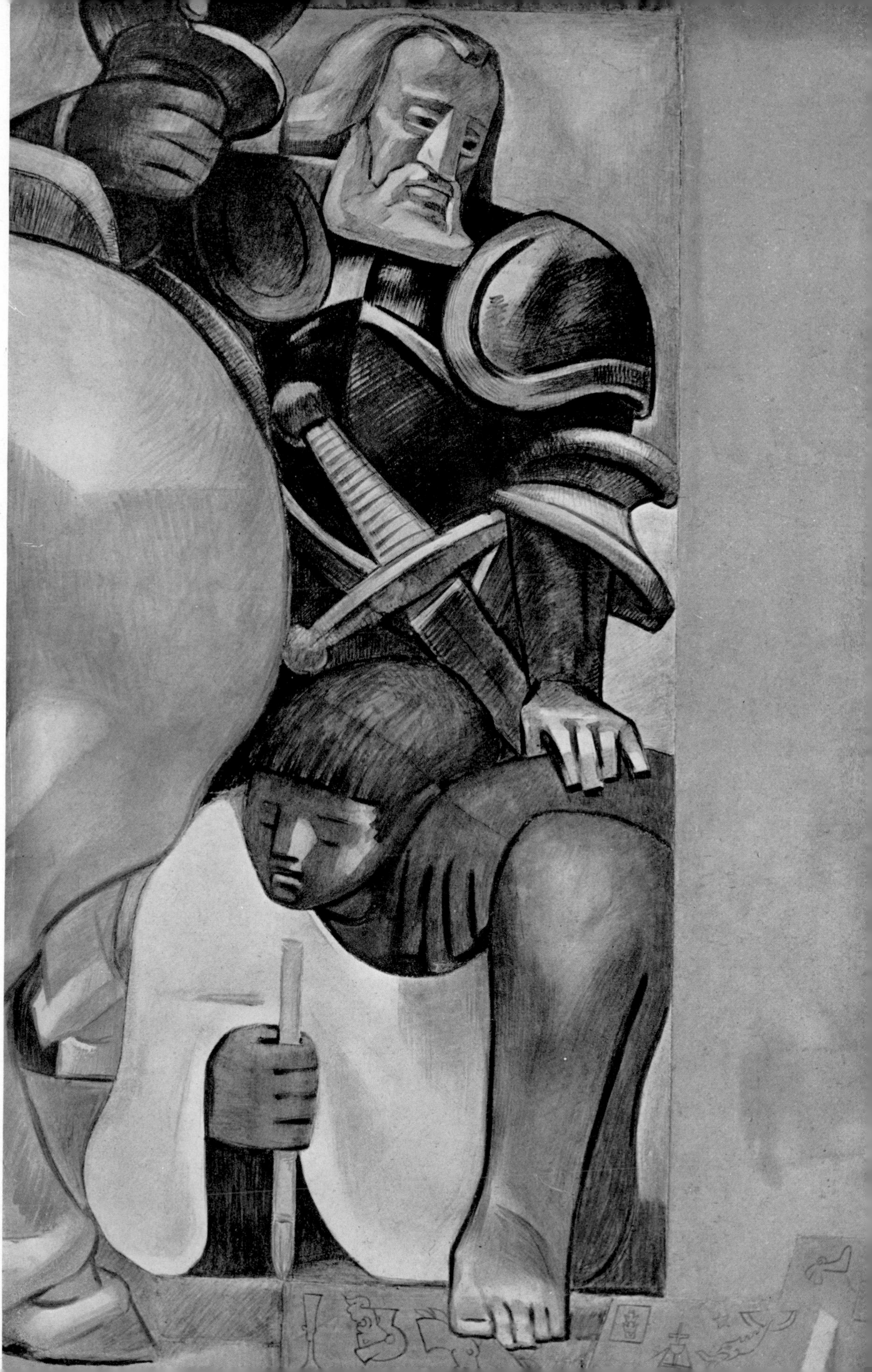

125 · *Cortez and an Indian Scribe · Fresco Detail · 1″=6½″*

126 · *Cartoon for Plate 127 · 19x25"*

Cortez

Indian Scribe

128 · *Head · Detail of Plate 125 · 1″ = 1 ¼″*

129 · *Foot* · *Detail of Plate 125* · *1″=1¼″*

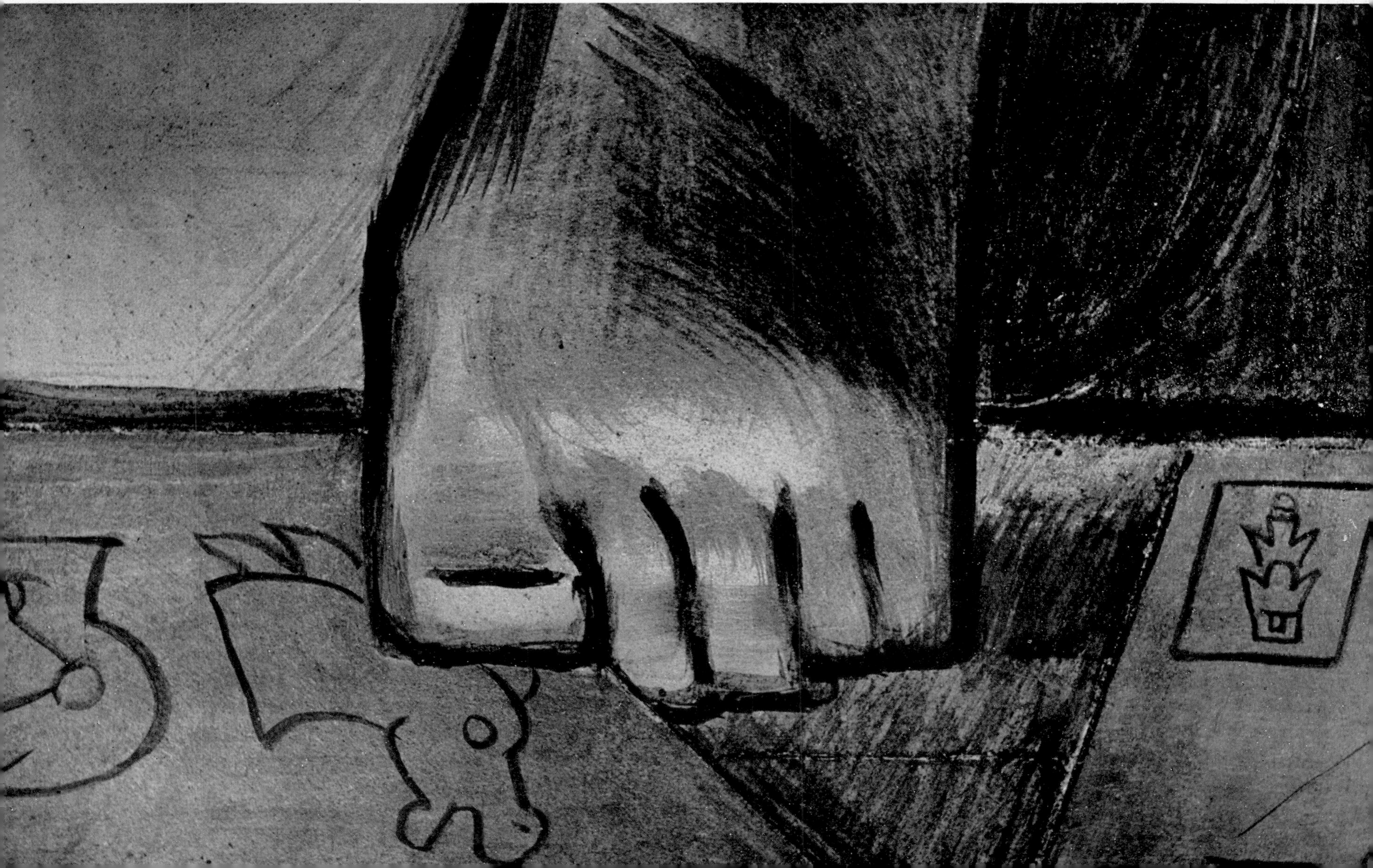

"TIME DISCLOSETH ALL THINGS"

131 · *Time's Puppets · Fresco Detail · 1"=4½"*

TIME DISCLOSETH ALL THINGS. The pause between panels is marked by the draped figure of a seated woman symbolizing Time in the same way that the medieval sculptor depicts the blissful souls bunched in a kerchief that patriarch Abraham holds against his bosom with wide open arms. All things that happen in time are cast together in Time's poke, the good with the bad: kings, emperors, poets, ku klux klans, scholars, painters, richmen, poormen, soldiers, a lamb beside a lion. The dove of peace perches outside, waiting for its turn to get in.

The bulging poke describes an inverted arch that bridges the gap between the two scenes and links the two painted arches into a single S line.

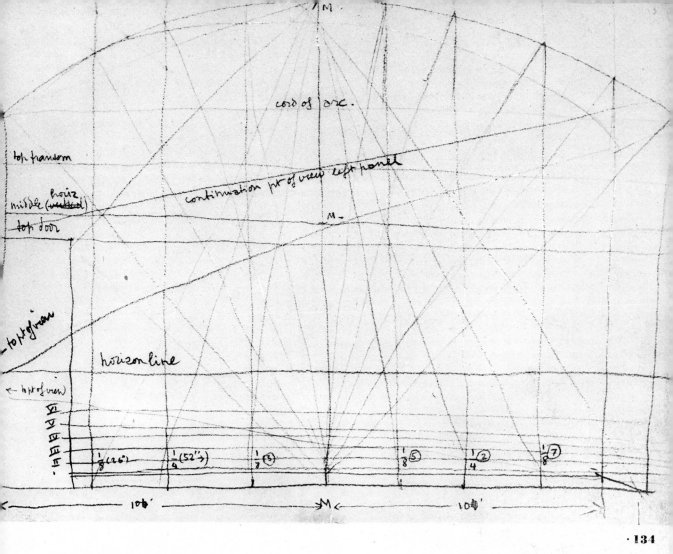

ANNO DMI. 1944. PRESS AND CAMERAMEN FLASH ON THE
SPOT NEWS. WORLD WAR II. The conquest of America, in its day a
bloody affair, brought Christianity to the new world. Today, against another background of turmoil and carnage, America frees Europe out of
Festung Europa.

The fresco depicts a demolition squad in action. Paratroopers loaded
with kits of dynamite land behind enemy lines. Men jump, tommy-guns
cradled in their arms, maneuver the chute risers towards a landing spot.

At left two men ease down the body of a third, landed atop a tree. At right the squad unpacks and mounts an 81 millimeter mortar as the commanding officer attempts to contact headquarters on his walkie-talkie.

Bundles still unopened lie on the ground, a red parachute trails behind medical supplies. Chutes still billowing or draped limp over bushes, unstrapped harnesses are the plastic dregs of action.

Reporters have jumped with the paratroopers and start typing their copy and taking "candid" shots even before they unhook their chute straps.

ANNO DEI 1944 · PRESS AND CAMERAMEN FLASH ON THE SPOT NEWS · WORLD WAR II

ear between Y of chin strap

in cold weather wooden underst zip to top and bu..

? emergen...
ad..

zip

stra
bac

strap
gaz mask

coot
pocket

gaz
mask

pant
pocket

strap gaz mas..

136 · Paratrooper · Drawn from Model · Fort Benning · 17x10"

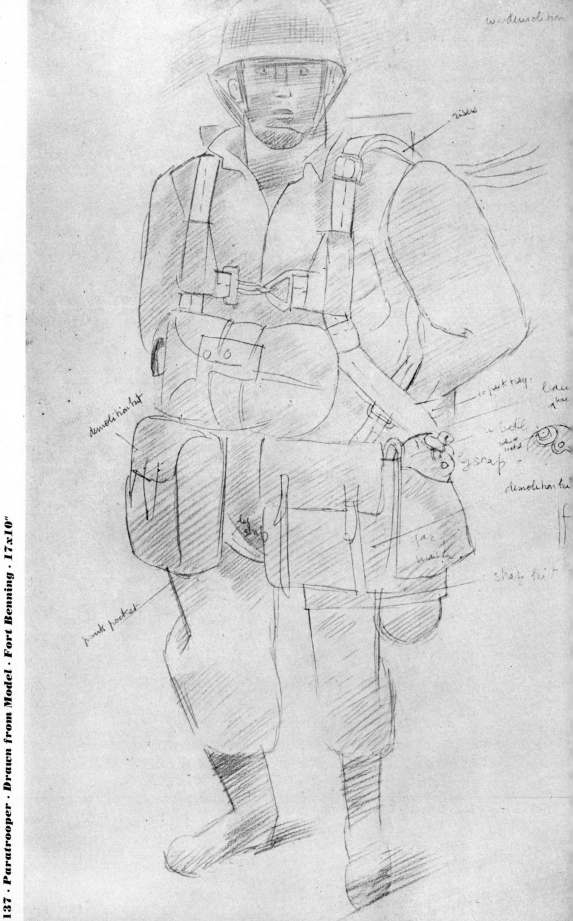

137 · *Paratrooper · Drawn from Model · Fort Benning · 17x10"*

138 · *First Idea · Pencil · 8½″ square*

'Deposition'

139 · *Fresco Detail · 1″=4¾″*

Typewriter

142 · *First Idea · Pencil · 9x8"*

Newsmen

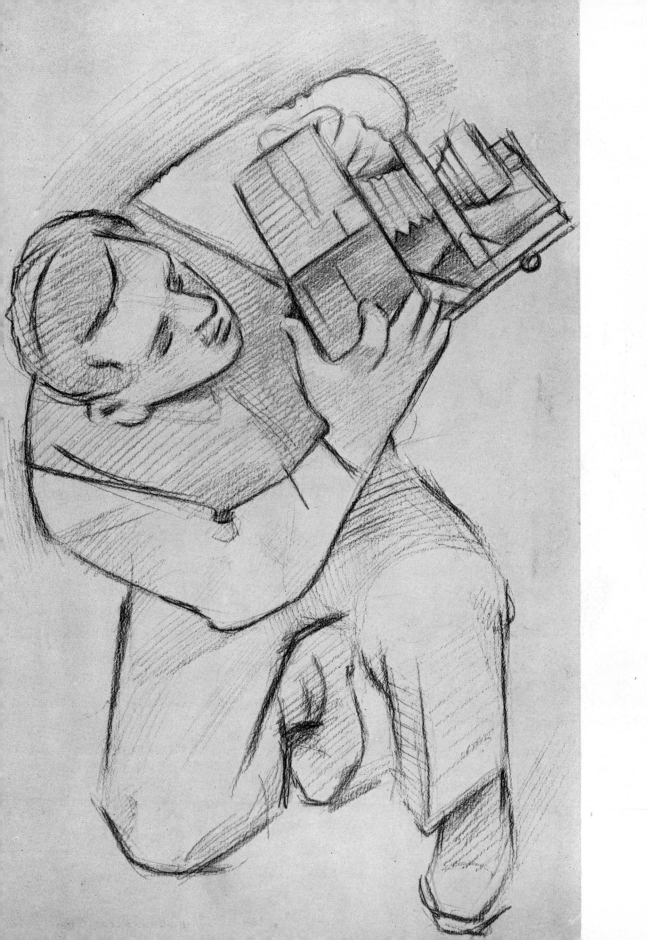

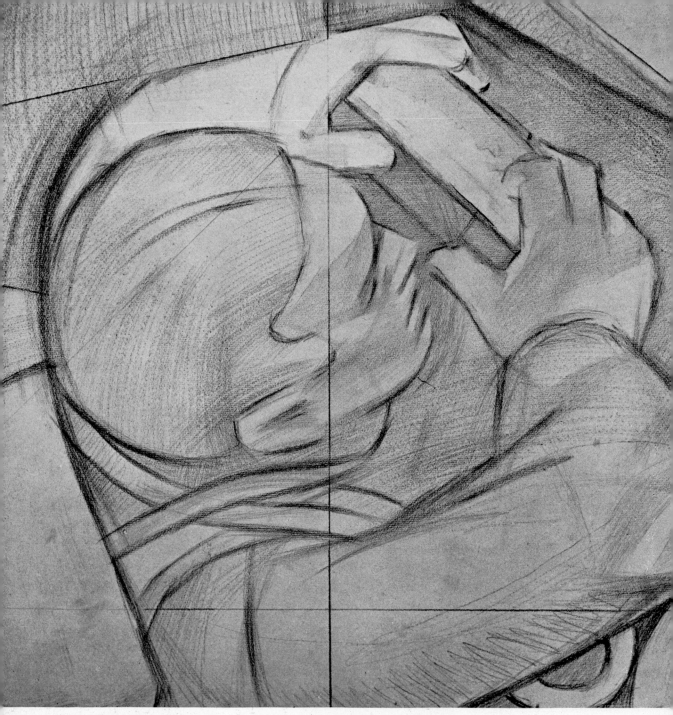

144 · *Cartoon Detail · Pencil*

Cameraman

◀ **146**
*Head · Drawn
from Model
8x6"*

147
*Hand · Drawn
from Model
4½x7"*
▼

148 · *Detail of Plate 149* · Fresco · 1"=1½"

150 · *First Paratrooper with Tommy-Gun · Drawn from Model · Fort Benning · 12x14"*

151 · *Cartoon Detail · Pencil · 19x25"*

First Paratrooper with Tommy-Gun

152 · *Fresco Final · 1"=4¼*

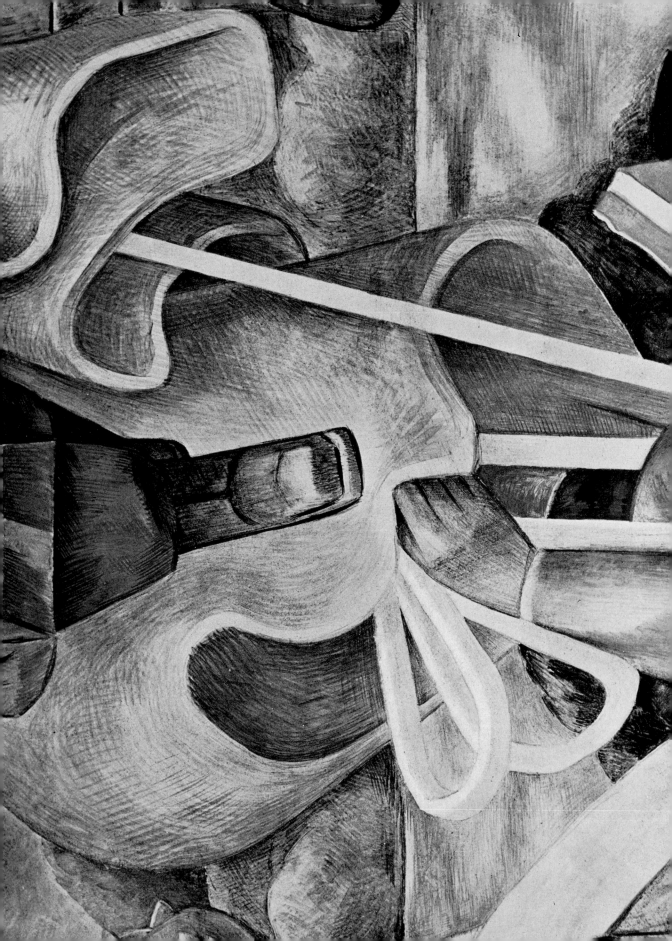

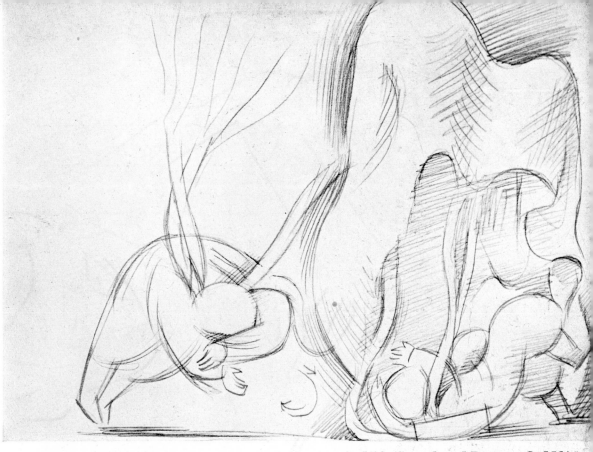

Falls · Action Sketches

154 · **Crouch and Bounce** · 8x11½"

155 · **Dragged on Belly** · 8x11½"

landing dragged on belly

156 · *Head Drawn from Model* · *Pencil* · *9x6"*

Fallen Paratrooper

157 · *Cartoon for Plate 158* · *Pencil* · *25x19"*

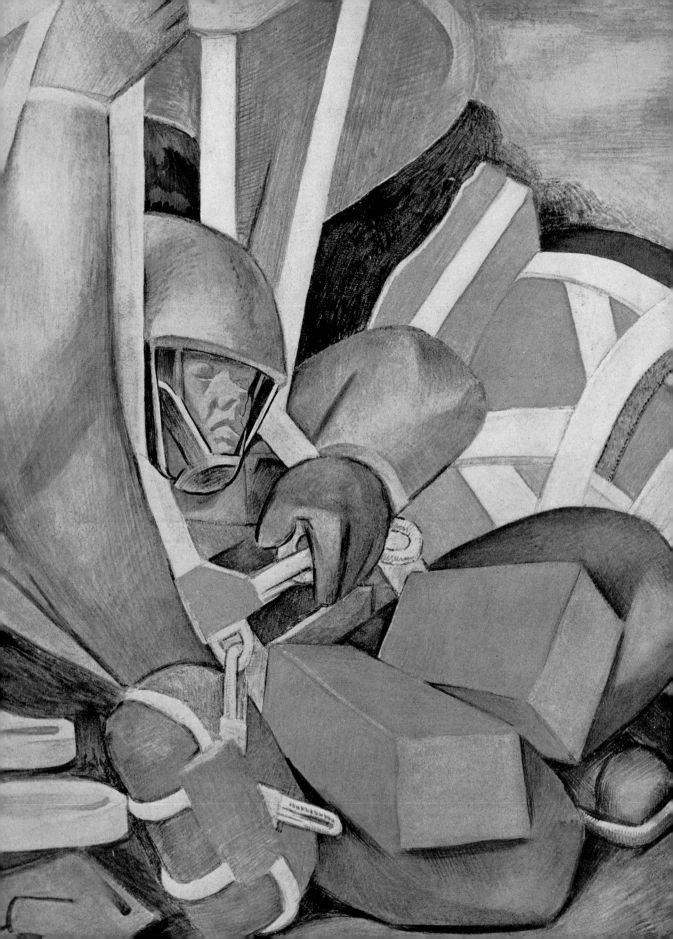

Fallen Paratrooper

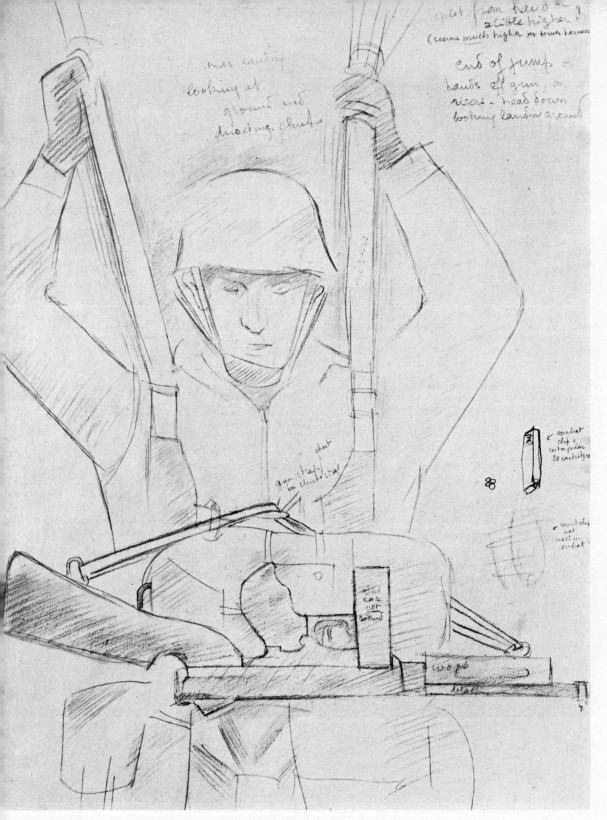

160 · Drawn from Model · 15x12" · Fort Benning

Second Paratrooper with Tommy-Gun

161 · First Sketch for Plate 133 · 11½x5"

Second Paratrooper with Tommy-Gun

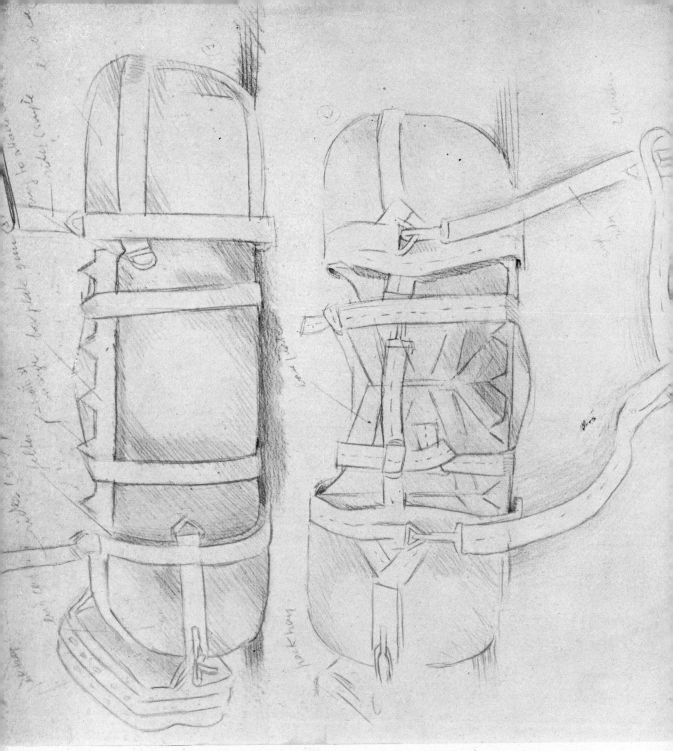

164 · Drawn from Nature · 12x12¾" · Fort Benning

Supply 'Bundles'

165 · Fresco Final · 1"=5"

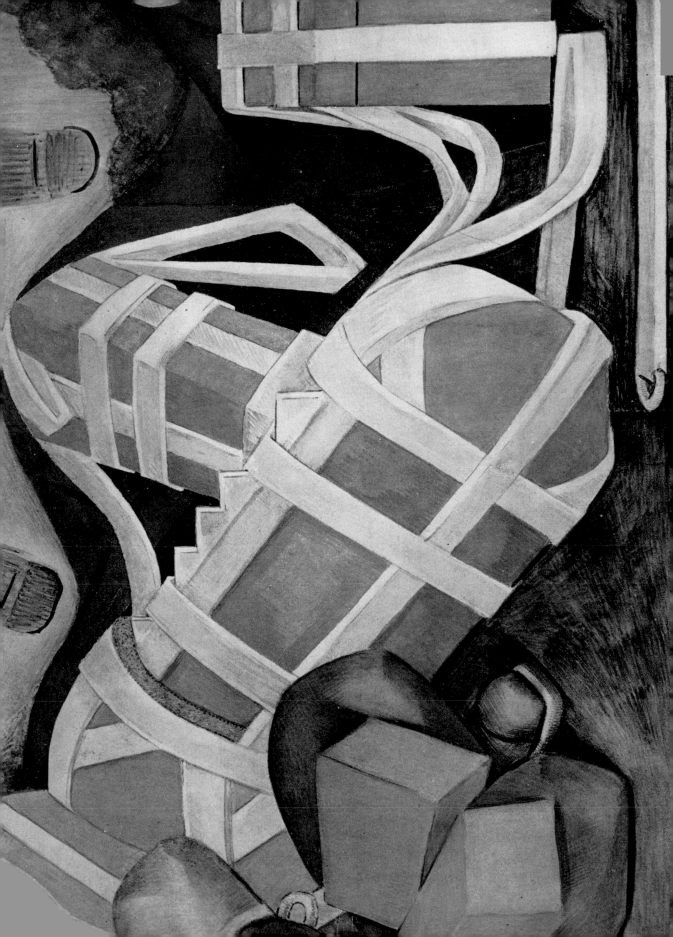

Fresco

Details

169 · *Man with Gun Barrel · Cartoon Detail · Pencil · 19x22"*

Mounting a Mortar

168 · *Man with Bipod · Cartoon Detail · Pencil · 19x12"*

172 · **Man with Base-Plate** · *Detail of Plate 170-171* · *1"=2'*

Mounting a Mortar

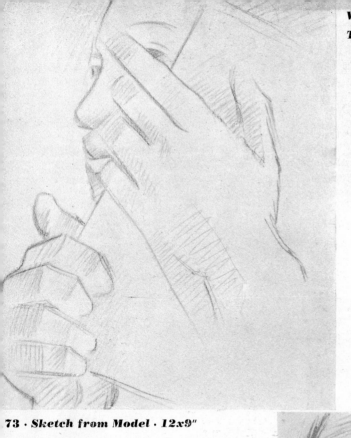

73 · Sketch from Model · 12x9"

174
First Idea
Pencil 12x9"

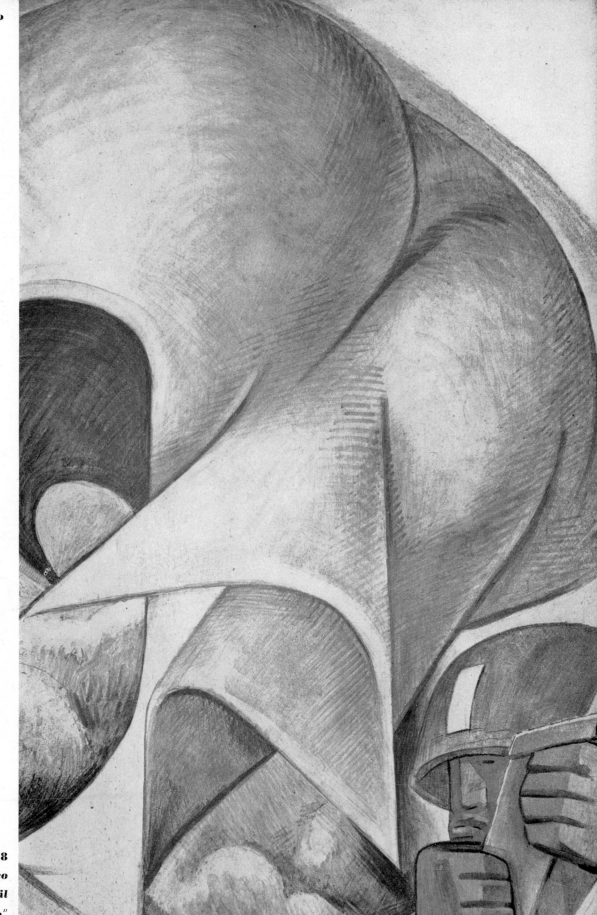

Walkie
Talkie

Twenty-five hundred copies of this book have been printed in the winter

of 1945 by Higgins-McArthur Co., Atlanta, Georgia. Format

and typography as suggested by Jean Charlot.

Plates by Aetna Photo-Engraving

Co., New York, N. Y.